# Wake Up, America!

What you need to know
about the War on Terror,
but are not being told by
your government or
the mainstream press.

# Wake Up, America!

What you need to know
about the War on Terror,
but are not being told by
your government or
the mainstream press.

(Written by an average citizen.)

For further information, please contact:
4299 Fox Trace, Boynton Beach, FL 33436
pfeaman@adelphia.com


Book designed by:
Arbor Books
19 Spear Road, Suite 301
Ramsey, NJ 07446
www.arborbooks.com


Printed in the United States of America


*Wake Up, America!*
Peter Feaman
National Security/Terrorism/Islam

1. Title  2. Author  3. Genre

Library of Congress Control Number: 2007925860

ISBN-10: 0-9795152-0-3
ISBN-13: 978-0-9795152-0-0

*Dedicated to:*
*My children and my children's children*

## Acknowledgements

To Synesio, who first inspired me to do this. To the Boca Raton Central Rotary Club, Bob and John, who inspired me along the way. To Maryanne, Linda and Barbara, for their tireless efforts.

To my wife Sally…and Uncle Bert.

# WAKE UP, AMERICA!
## Understanding Jihad for dummies!

## Table of Contents

# PRE-FOREWORD

To all Muslims who are people of peace; to all Muslims who would like to peacefully co-exist in the same country or society with non-Muslims; to all Muslims in the U.S. who peacefully live in America and participate in the Rotary, Kiwanis or any number of non-denominational service organizations that can be found in Anytown, U.S.A.: this book is not critical of you. It is a plea, however, for you to speak out, to renounce radical Islam, and to renounce murder and beheadings in the name of your religion.

Nor is this book intended to invite Americans to view all Muslims with suspicion. Tolerance, however, is a two-way street. Muslims immigrating to our country should be tolerant of the customs and practices of Americans developed over two centuries of this American experiment in freedom. This includes the freedom to criticize some parts of the Muslim religion that contradict our traditional notions of the sanctity of human life, the equality of opportunity for men and women, and to support the notion that we are all "endowed by (our) Creator with certain unalienable Rights, (including) Life, Liberty and the pursuit of Happiness."

Finally, for those who fear that books such as this will foster racism and bigotry, I suggest that such sentiment underestimates the fundamental goodness of the American people. Any Muslim that joins in the call for the reformation of radical Islam will be applauded.

# FOREWORD

Soon after 9/11, all of the focus was on the apprehension of Osama bin Laden as the mastermind of the horrific murders that occurred that day.

We have since learned that bin Laden's capture will not end the terror threats the world faces.

There is a monster on the loose about which neither the mainstream press nor the Bush administration is adequately informing us. It's been called Islamofascism, Radical Islam and Islamic Fundamentalism. Whatever you name it, it is an ideology that has killed tens of thousands around the globe in the last few years and threatens all of us, today.

It is killing thousands in Ethiopia, Somalia, the Sudan, Malaysia, Indonesia, Thailand and the Philippines, not to mention the train bombings in Spain, the train and bus bombings in London and the riots in France. In this book:

- You will read some of what the news media is not telling you about the War on Terror.
- You will read how Europe, as we know it, will disappear in our lifetime.
- You will read how "Tolerance is cultural suicide when it's a one-way street."
- You will ask yourself the most important question of all: *Will Judeo-Christianity Survive?*

Finally, as this book goes to press, Congress has passed the war funding bill setting deadlines for the withdrawal of troops from Iraq. Such a policy is naive and dangerous.

# CHAPTER 1

# WHAT THE NEWS MEDIA IS NOT TELLING US ABOUT THE WAR ON TERROR

*"Those ignorant of history are doomed to repeat it."*

## THE CLASH OF CIVILIZATIONS

It's not like it used to be. In revolutionary times, Paul Revere was able to ride on his horse, warning the townsfolk outside of Boston, "The British are coming!" The townsfolk could then look out into the harbor, see the tall ships, the Union Jack, and prepare accordingly.

When Fort Sumter was fired upon, the beginning of the War Between the States had begun, and the battle lines were very clearly marked, geographically and politically.

When Pearl Harbor was attacked, the enemy states were obvious and World War II began for the U.S. as our fathers and grandfathers took up arms to defeat the fascists that threatened our freedom and our way of life.

Now, two generations after Pearl Harbor, we are again in a war; and it is a war, in my view, for the survival of Western Civilization. A war to keep the freedoms and prosperity which our Western Civilization has brought. That might have been considered an overstatement to the casual observer until February, 2006. Now all the world has seen, and especially the West, one would hope, that our fundamental freedoms that we in the West take for granted, (i.e. freedom of speech, freedom of the press, and freedom of religion) are under direct attack. I am referring, of course, to the worldwide rioting that mushroomed overnight in response to the publication of the so-called offensive cartoons published in a Danish newspaper. Unfortunately, the reaction of media outlets throughout the world to the Muslim cartoon rioting sent the wrong message. The response was to cease publishing the "offensive" material, thereby validating the Muslim demand of censorship and the abolition of free speech. More recently in Europe (Germany to be specific) a performance of Mozart music was cancelled for fear of offending Muslims. The concert was recently rescheduled. Tolerance, however, is cultural suicide when it's a one-way street (see Chapter 6).

In September, 2006 it was a speech by Pope Benedict that ignited global Muslim outrage once again. Some radical Muslims even declared a "Fatwa" against the Pope. (Permission to kill the Pope as an acceptable response to the Pope's quotation of a fourteenth century Byzantine Emperor) What? On Tuesday, September 19, 2006, an Associated Press article reported that Al-Qaeda in Iraq warned Pope Benedict XVI that its "war against Christianity and the West will go on until Islam takes over the world…" Simultaneously, Iran's supreme leader called for more protest over the Pope's remarks on Islam. As with other so called "insults" to Islam, protests broke out not just in the Middle East, but in South Asia and Indonesia. In the Middle East, demonstrators carrying black flags burned an effigy of the Pope.

As we should have learned from dealing with fascism in the past, appeasement or capitulation to those who seek to repress others or their freedoms will only lead to more demands, more repression and increased fascism. Neville Chamberlain promised "peace in our time," after agreeing to Hitler's demands in 1939. The invasion of Poland thereafter should remind us all that appeasement in the face of evil does not work. Those ignorant of history are doomed to repeat it.

The danger is that the warning signs of this epic struggle for the survival of Western Civilization and the Judeo-Christian ethic continue to be ignored by our politicians and media elite.

The warnings signs began long before "9/11." The Islamic Revolution in Iran in 1979 marked the beginning of what some have called, "World War IV." (W.W. III being the struggle against, and conquest of, Communism in the West.).

After the bombing of the U.S. Marine barracks in Beirut, the World Trade Center bombing in 1993 was the first attack here in the U.S. Unfortunately, the act of war was treated like a criminal event, rather than the first shot over the bow in a global conflict between two civilizations holding polar opposite values. As a result, the terrorists were emboldened, and a few years later, two of our embassies in Africa were bombed. Again, the U.S. took little action, treating the bombings as isolated criminal events.

In 2000, our Navy ship, the U.S.S. Cole was bombed, killing a few dozen United States sailors. A few dozen sailors! And yet, we as a nation yawned. The Spanish-American War of 1898 began because of the sabotage of the Maine in Havana harbor in the country of Cuba. "Remember the Maine!" was the cry that empowered and emboldened a nation. Teddy Roosevelt and his Rough Riders fought for a sense of purpose and righteousness. Today, when the U.S.S. Cole was attacked there was no collective moral outrage.

Finally, in a sneak attack more deadly than Pearl Harbor, on September 11, 2001, over 3,000 innocent people were killed as the World Trade Center in New York, the greatest symbol of vibrant capitalism in the western world, was destroyed. America finally took action, and the fronts have now shifted. I say "fronts" in the plural because the war rages in many places, not just in Iraq and Afghanistan.

## THE ISLAMOFASCIST WAR IN EUROPE
The importance of Europe to our cultural survival cannot be overlooked. The train bombing in Spain changed the

results of its presidential election, and now Spain can no longer be trusted as an ally in the war on terror. The <u>externaly</u> Islamofascist war in Europe has begun and is in full swing. The 30-year-old <u>internal</u> war in Europe is discussed in Chapter 2.

On November 2, 2004, on a street in Amsterdam, Theo Van Gogh, a descendent of the great Dutch painter, was bicycling to work. He had produced, directed and broadcast a film about Islamic violence against Islamic women. On that cold, grey European day, a Dutch-Moroccan Muslim shot Van Gogh off his bicycle. As Van Gogh lay dying in the street, he pleaded for his life. The assassin responded by shooting him again, after which he slit Van Gogh's throat and stabbed a knife into his chest with a letter attached. The letter said, in part, "I surely know that you, Oh America, will be destroyed. I surely know that you, Oh Europe, will be destroyed. I surely know that you, Oh Holland, will be destroyed."[i]

In Germany, Muslim students approved of Van Gogh's murder, saying, "If you insult Islam, you have to pay."[ii] This reaction was not a surprise to those who have been observing German culture over the preceding 20 years. The seeds of this German reaction had been sewn years before. In 2002, a German constitutional court ruled that the German school system in Berlin must teach its Muslim students, who are the majority population in an elementary school, a Muslim curriculum. After that ruling, a letter was written to the local newspaper:

> "Germany is an Islamic country. Islam is in the home, in schools. Germans will be

outnumbered. We (Muslims) will say what
we want, will live how we want. It's outra-
geous that Germans demand we speak their
language. Our children will have our
language, our laws, our culture." [iii]

The British train and bus bombings that took place in
the summer of 2005 spread the war across the
Channel. Back on the other side, in the fall of 2005,
French authorities confronted rioters throughout the
country. Contrary to how the press reported it as
"poor vs. rich," the riots were a Muslim community
rising up. Note the headline appearing in the *Sun
Sentinel* on November 25, 2005: "French Fear Riots
Could Fuel Discontent - Some Predict Movement to
Islamic Jihad." [iv] That "Movement" started years ago
and is now in full swing.

On New Year's Eve, 2006, France was still under
Marshal Law. A short newspaper article appearing in
the *Sun Sentinel* on December 31, 2005 declared that
France had deployed 25,000 troops to quell suspected
rioting and that the entire country was still under a
dusk to dawn curfew. [v]

It is no accident that France and Germany failed to
support the United States in its military response to
terror in Afghanistan or Iraq. The fact that both countries benefited monetarily by keeping Saddam
Hussein in power only tells part of the story. Europe
is in the process of becoming an Islamic colony.
*"Eurabia*—The Euro-Arab Axis" by Bat Ye'or, states
in Chapter One, entitled "Eurabia Revealed":

In her forceful book, *"La Forza della Ragione,"* (The Force of Reason) Oriana Fallaci ponders the steady Islamization of Europe noting "it was all there for years and we didn't see it." This "all there" relates to burning questions. Why have generations of Europeans been taught in universities to despise America and harbor an implacable hatred for Israel? Why has the European Union (EU) proposed a constitution that willingly renounces and even denies its Judeo-Christian roots? Has the 1930's—World War II alliance of Arab Jihad with European Nazis and fascists been resurrected today? [vi]

The answer is yes. (See Chapter 2—"The Islamization of Europe.")

## THE ISLAMOFASCIST WAR IN THE FAR EAST

The report appearing the day after Christmas, December 26, 2005, written by the Associated Press and published on FoxNews.com stated:

"Masked, black-clad and brandishing machetes, the attackers sprang from behind the screen of tall grass and pounced on the four Christian girls as they walked to school. Within seconds, three of the teenagers were beheaded—fresh victims of violence that has turned this Indonesian island into yet another front in the terrorist wars. Sulawesi is one of several islands in what some call Southeast Asia's Triangle of Terror, a region encompassing the insurgency-racked southern Philippines in the North and the Malacou Archipelago, itself a scene of sectarian conflict to the West and close by is heavily Muslim southern Thailand where a two-year insurgency has left more than 1,100 dead. Muslim Christian violence from 2000 to 2003 killed some 1,000 people in Sulawesi and attracted Muslim militants from across Indonesia,… and even from the distant Middle East." [vii]

But you won't see this reported in the mainstream media outlets. The Far East, from Thailand to the Philippines, struggles daily with Islamofascist violence, yet the violence goes largely unreported in the press.

## THE ISLAMOFASCIST WAR IN AFRICA
### Nigeria

In Nigeria, Muslim radicals have targeted mainly Christians but the violence has been widespread and deadly, largely unreported by the mainstream media.

### Sudan and Chad

Slowly, world attention has been

increasingly drawn to the civil war in the Sudan which is now spilling over into Chad. What has not been reported is the fact that the "Arab" insurgents are militant Islamofascists engaged in the systematic destruction of the Christian people of southern Sudan. Although the slaughter has been reported, it has not been reported as Muslims vs. Christians, which is, in fact, the case.

## THE ISLAMOFASCIST WAR IN THE MIDDLE EAST

Obviously, the most active front in our war against Islamofascism is Iraq. Al-Qaeda is in Iraq and the bitter internal struggle now being fought there is truly a war between moderate Muslims and Islamofascists. Should that struggle be lost to the radical Islamofascists, Iran is poised to become the dominant player in the Middle East. To make matters worse, Iranian President Mahmoud Ahmadinejad has become the spokesperson and world leader of the Islamofascists. We are in the process of witnessing Islamofascism transfer itself from a terrorist organization, operating as a rogue state, into a government-led, state-sponsored terrorist war machine. An Islamofascist militarized state, such as Iran, actively seeking nuclear weapons reveals that the hunt for Osama Bin Laden is only a very small part of the overall war on Islamofascism. Capturing bin Laden would no more end our "War on Terror" than capturing Mussolini ended World War II. President Ahmadinejad called Israel a "permanent threat" to the

Middle East that will "soon" be liberated. "Like it or not, the Zionist regime is heading toward annihilation... The Zionist regime is a rotten, dry tree that will be eliminated by one storm."[viii] As Iran seeks nuclear capability, it's not hard to figure out what that "one storm" might be. President Ahmadinejad has stated "Israel must be wiped off the map" and that "the existence of this (Israel) regime is a permanent threat to the Middle East. Its existence has harmed the dignity of Islamic nations."

Further, what the mainstream news media has <u>not</u> discussed with any clarity is what President Ahmadinejad has said about the United States and others. Ahmadinejad, in the same statement, referenced above, called for "eliminating the United States from the world" and backing terrorism against any <u>Muslim country</u> that made peace with Israel.[ix] The latest developments in Iran show that its government continues to defy the West and the U.N. by continuing to enrich uranium for "energy production." Yet, Iran sits on the world's second largest supply of oil, second only to that of Saudi Arabia. Can anyone seriously accept Iran's claims that it seeks nuclear capability for only peaceful purposes? Of course not.

The warning signs are all around us. We are at war. But this war cannot be won unless we **<u>specifically identify the enemy</u>**.

## DEFINING THE ENEMY

The problem (not properly defining the enemy) began when the Bush Administration, after 9/11, characterized the conflict we now face as a "War on Terror." We are not fighting a "War on Terror" any more than if the World Trade Center and the Pentagon had been bombed by B-52s flying at 40,000 feet, the conflict would be called the "War on High Flying B-52s!"

Terror describes <u>the method of attack</u>, not who attacked us or <u>who</u> we, the West, are at war with.

Terrorism is caused by people—people with a certain ideology, and if we can't identify them, we certainly can't defeat them. So who <u>is</u> the enemy the West faces?

On Saturday, February 18, 2006, Bridgette Gabriel delivered a speech at the Intelligence Summit in Washington, D.C. She stated:

> "The most important element of intelligence has to be understanding the mindset and intention of the enemy. The West has been wallowing in a state of ignorance and denial for thirty years, as Muslim extremists perpetuated evil against innocent victims in the name of Allah... America cannot effectively defend itself in this war unless and until the American people understand the nature of the enemy that we face. We are fighting a powerful ideology that is capable of altering human basic instincts. An ideology that can turn a mother into a launching pad of death. A perfect example is a recently elected Hamas official in the Palestinian territories who raves

in heavenly joy about sending her three sons to death and offering the ones who are still alive for the cause." [x]

The enemy that we face are "Islamofascists." Chuck Colson on his website, Breakpoint.org., as well as many others, has adopted this label. The media, because they don't "get it," will resist this. (See Chapter 4) In fact, President Bush, in speaking on the occasion of the fifth anniversary of the 9/11 murders, finally identified the enemy as "Islamic Fascists." After the predictable expressions of outrage by American Muslims, mainstream media outlets, and leftist politicians, the President abandoned the term, leaving the American people still adrift in a sea of moral vagueness about who we are fighting and why. If our leaders, excluding former Senator Rick Santorum from Pennsylvania, would forcefully articulate <u>who</u> the enemy is and <u>why</u> we fight, I believe enough Americans would rally around the cause of freedom and self-preservation to support the present foreign policy of the United States.

So, just who are these Islamofascists?

They are Muslim extremists who, driven by a totalitarian political ideology, that, like Communism and Nazism before it, are determined to destroy freedom and the institutions that support it, and then enslave or kill those people who disagree. All doubt of this has now been erased by observing the conduct of Islamofascists across the globe in response to the publishing of the editorial cartoons that were supposedly insensitive to Muslim beliefs.

I suggest "political correctness" is preventing politicians and policy-makers from declaring war on "Islamofascists," so as not to offend Islamic moderates. This concern is unnecessary. Why? Since 2002, the United States has invaded, occupied and, by force of arms, overthrown two Muslim nations. Those Muslims who are susceptible of being offended by the actions of the U.S. are already offended by now![xi] Therefore, our leaders must publicly identify our enemy—Islamofascists.

So, the next question to be asked is: *What is the ideology of an Islamofascist?*

Most Islamofascists believe in the power of the state to sponsor and impose the Islamic religious code known as the "Sharia" on all of its citizens. Such a government is a "church-state" that contemplates no separation of church and state, and tolerates no freedom of thought, freedom of press, or freedom of religion. This is borne out by the February, 2006 demonstrations that openly proclaimed, "Anyone who insults Islam must die," and various other endearing slogans. This should leave no doubt to even radical leftists like Michael Moore that, had George Bush been a Muslim, Michael Moore would have long since been beheaded.[xii]

The great concern, and largely ignored by the media, is that Islamofascist states are growing and are on the move. Saudi Arabia was the first Islamofascist state and it continues today. You will find no churches or synagogues in that country. Other Islamofascist states include Iran, Palestine (made even worse by the election of Hamas), Libya, Egypt…increasingly, Turkey…increasingly, Northern Nigeria, the Sudan, Syria, Indonesia, and parts of Thailand. Largely unreported by the press is the current Islamofascist civil war in the Philippines.

## IRAN

Today, you hear the President of Iran, Mahmoud Ahmadinejad state that he wishes to wipe Israel off the face of the map. In September, 2006, addressing the U.N. General Assembly in New York, Ahmadinejad prayed for the Islamic messiah to usher in an era of world peace and the conversion of all peoples to Islam. The unspoken prayer was that, according to Muslim beliefs, the appearance of the Muslim messiah is preceded by a world-wide conflict wherein the world is cleansed of all "infidels." Note: Any non- Muslim is an "infidel." It is obvious that neither our political leaders or the mainstream press is connecting the dots. By stringing together into one paragraph the various quotes of not only Ahmadinejad but other Islamic fascists around the world, there is an ongoing clarion call for the imposition of Islamic rule worldwide, by force of arms or otherwise. Even more clearly, a war <u>has</u> been declared against not only Israel and the United States, but the West.

It all seems eerily similar to Germany in the 1920's and 30's. The strategy of a radical minority intimidating a non-radical majority is the same process that took place in Germany in the pre- World War II decades. Like the Nazis who intimidated moderate Germans, first into silence, then collaboration, and ultimately full support; so the moderate Muslim world is intimidated into silence and, in many quarters, full support of the radical Islamofascists and their terrorist activities. Poor and disenfranchised Muslim youths in Europe and elsewhere form a perfect Petri dish in which Islamofascists recruit and grow an ideology of hate; an ideology and indoctrination which they hope will culminate in a worldwide revolution of Islamofascism. Those ignorant of history are doomed to repeat it.

If there is one thing we should have learned from those dark years of pre-World War II Germany: when a head of state says that they want to kill you, believe them, and take action before it's too late.

## PALESTINE

The election of Hamas as the governing body of Palestine in 2006 is most revealing. The following is a quote from Hamas leader Khaled Mash'al at a mosque in Damascus in February, 2006:

> "Today the Arab and Islamic nation is rising and awakening and it will reach its peak, Allah willing. It will be victorious. It will link the present to the past. It will open the horizons of the future. It will regain the leadership of the world. Allah willing, the day is not far off... this victory which was clearly evident in the election, conveys a message to

Israel, to America and to all the oppressors around the world: today you are fighting the Army of Allah. You are fighting against peoples for whom death for the sake of Allah and for the sake of honor and glory is preferable to life. You are fighting a nation that does not tire, even after 1,000 years of fighting... Before Israel dies, it must be humiliated and degraded." [xiii]

The crowd then shouts "death to Israel, death to Israel, death to America."

We cannot wage a war against Islamofascists while:
a.   Our leaders and the mainstream media are unwilling to identify the enemy.
b.   Maintaining our dependence on foreign oil. Oil money flows daily into the coffers of the Islamofascists and feeds the beast that grows and becomes more ferocious with every gallon of Middle East oil that is bought and sold.
c.   Turning a blind eye to Islamic destruction of Hindus, Christians and other "infidels" around the world, not just in the Middle East.
d.   Allowing mass immigration of Muslims and others into our own country, which, if not controlled, will dilute our sense of who we are as a nation and our role in world affairs.

e.  Allowing "political correctness" to intimidate or blind us from recognizing and dealing with the threat America faces.

# CHAPTER 2
# THE ISLAMIZATION OF EUROPE

*WINSTON CHURCHILL, WHERE ARE YOU?*

In what might be called a demographic "perfect storm," Europe, as we know it, will cease to exist in thirty years.

In Chapter 1, you read the chilling account of the murder of Theo Van Gogh in Amsterdam. This gives rise to greater research in an effort to find out what is going on in the land of our forefathers and the lands from which our laws, culture and heritage descended. The results are shocking.

The confluence of three events or trends intersecting in Europe is causing the demise of a civilization that, for eight hundred years, has led the planet in political, scientific and spiritual thought; a civilization that took the world from the Dark Ages to the post-modern era. That millennium, led by the Judeo-Christian thought of the Western world, took the human race to its greatest longevity in life span, to its lowest infant mortality rate and more advances in science, technology and human dignity than the world had ever seen.

That reign of Europe is now over.

## EVENT NO. 1: THE BIRTH DEARTH

The European twentieth century witnessed two wars so horrific, in two successive generations, that these conflicts alone might have caused the decline and fall of that civilization and culture.

The U.S. recovered from World War II because soldiers returned home from the war and had babies, lots of them, creating the "baby boom" generation, of which this author is one. However, no such demographic explosion occurred in Europe. In American cities, homes and infrastructure remained intact, and in 1946 Americans simply went back to work in a peace-time economy. In Europe, the people had to start, literally, from scratch. The re-builders faced destroyed farms and villages, decimated cities, no infrastructure, but worse, no determined people bent on re-populating the continent.

Although Europeans rebuilt their infrastructure, there arose a parallel intellectual re-examination of themselves. This academic review soon turned cannibalistic. It resulted in an intellectual European self-recrimination, and grew to such an extent that a tremendous anti-Western stream of thought took root within the European academic elite. Among other consequences after World War II, there was no significant baby-boom generation in Europe. Continuously, for the last fifty years Europeans have simply decided not to have children. These demographic events are pushing Europe into oblivion, while its academic and political elites are accelerating this demise with their own brand of cultural suicide.

Here are some demographic statistics:

Note: A birth rate of 2.1 children per couple is needed for a population simply to at least maintain itself.

The birthrates across much of Europe reveal a culture unwilling to reproduce itself in order to survive in the long term.

In France—The birth rate is 1.8 and because of immigration, one-third of all babies born in France are of Muslim parents.

In Belgium—the birth rate is now 1.2 and fifty percent of all babies born in Belgium today are of Muslim parents.

In Germany—the birth rate is 1.3. In the next twenty years, Germany will lose one-third of its native population.

In Spain, Italy and Russia it is even worse. In Italy the birth rate is 1.2, in Russia 1.17 and in Spain, an astounding 1.07.

Europe, as a whole, has a birth rate of 1.4. As a result, Europe will lose one hundred twenty-eight million (128,000,000) indigenous people by the year

2050. This demographic demise is worse even than the black plague that struck Europe in 1347.[xiv]

But the loss of the European indigenous population *will be replaced*. They will be replaced by immigrants. And who will these immigrants be and who have they been?

## EVENT NO. 2: MUSLIM IMMIGRATION

The second event of this demographic perfect storm has been Muslim immigration into Europe during the last sixty years.

In 1945, Europe began the process of post-World War II reconstruction. It needed great numbers of "guest workers" in order to rebuild. For forty years they came by the hundreds of thousands from places like Turkey, Morocco and Tunisia, and overwhelming, they were Muslim.

The first Muslim immigrants came without their families. But things did not work out as expected by the European leaders who first conceived of the "guest worker" plan. The Muslim "guest" status changed quickly. Wives soon followed the workers that came. The predictable result was, of course, children. The Guest Visas then turned into Permanent Visas. Then more children arrived, great numbers of them Muslims: but now, born in old Europe as European citizens.

But this immigrant explosion was different from what we here in the United States experienced when our periods of great immigrations took place. Unlike the Irish, Italians, Jews from all over the world, Koreans, and Vietnamese, all of whom assimilated and blended into a uniquely American culture, the Muslims in Europe did not, and are not, assimilating into the European culture. In fact, it is just the opposite. [xv] In Berlin, Germany young immigrant women have been murdered by family members—for, well, behaving like Germans. What German behavior is so offensive so as to merit a death sentence, to be carried out by members of the offender's own family? Wearing western style clothing and allowing the female sibling to be alone with another single male was the offense. This conduct so embarrassed and humiliated the family, she was allowed to be murdered by her brothers. Has multicultural tolerance helped create a parallel society in the heart of Europe? [xvi]

Europe would do well to imitate the American model of immigration as first espoused by Theodore Roosevelt in 1907:

> "In the first place, we should insist that if the immigrant who comes here in good faith, becomes an American and assimilates himself to us, he shall be treated on an exact equality with everyone else, for it is an outrage to discriminate against any such man because of creed, or birth place, or origin. But this is predicated upon the person's becoming in every facet an American, and nothing but an American...

There can be no divided allegiance here. Any man who says he is an American, but something else also, isn't an American at all. We have room for but one flag, the American flag... We have room for but one language here, and that is the English language... and we have room for but one sole loyalty and that is a loyalty to the American people." [xvii]

But the Europeans have not adopted the American model.

As Europe becomes "more tolerant" and "sensitive," the Muslims increase their demands for a separate culture and separate laws. For example, for twenty years, the Islamic Federation of Berlin struggled in the courts to secure Islamic religious instruction in public elementary schools. In 2001 they succeeded. Based upon a German constitutional court ruling, today <u>thousands</u> of children in Berlin are taught by teachers hired by the Islamic Federation and paid with taxpayer money. Because of political correctness, instructors hold lessons in Turkish or Arabic, BEHIND CLOSED DOORS. [xviii]

Then there is the story of the former Dutch member of Parliament who tired of living under twenty-four hour security in a government-owned apartment complex because of her perceived anti-Muslim opinions. She has resigned her seat in the Parliament and is taking up residence in the United States. [xix]

In and of itself, Muslim immigration would not pose a threat to western values and the West's concepts of freedom of speech, freedom of the press and freedom of religion. However, as we witness the worldwide rioting, murder and mayhem invoked in reaction to the publication of an editorial cartoon deemed offensive to Muslim dogma, or statements by the Pope (or anyone else for that matter) who dares to insult Islam, the danger becomes real. Some of the placards displayed and chants recited during the riots that took place all over the world turned the western concept of tolerance on its head:

"Behead Those Who Insult Islam.",

"Europe, you will pay, extermination is on the way.",

"Butcher those who mock Islam."

The signs warn Europeans of their own impending 9/11: "Europe: your 9/11 will come." [xx]

This brand of Islamofascism *does* threaten Western ideals of freedom of the press, religion and speech.

## EVENT NO. 3
## THE RISE OF JIHAD OR ISLAMOFASCISM

Modern Islamofascism ("modern" because this is not the first time since the advent of the Muslim religion that Islamofascism has been a force of destruction. See Chapter 3) began in 1979 with the fall of the Shah of Iran and the coming to power of the Ayatollah Khomeini, accompanied by the abduction of the American Embassy hostages.

Some of the highlights (or lowlights) of Jihad in Europe since 9/11:

The train bombings in Spain.

The murder of Theo Van Gogh in Holland.

The subway and bus bombings in London.

The Muslim riots in France before Christmas, 2005.

The outrage of Islamofascists over the cartoon of Mohammad with a bomb for a turban, appearing in a Danish newspaper.

The outrage of Islamofascists in reaction to Pope Benedict's speech intended to promote interfaith dialogue, where the Pope's murder is now called for.

———————

These events in Europe bring to the fore and crystallize the ongoing global clash of civilizations and, more specifically, the growing conflict in Europe. The violence is only a harbinger of things to come. The "Jihad" declared by Iranian President Ahmadinejad against Israel and the West is loosely translated as "my struggle." In the German language, "my struggle" is translated into the words "Mien Kempf."

This is how it all started 75 years ago in Nazi Germany. The winds of war are blowing once again as our freedoms come under attack. And now in Europe, their freedom of the press and freedom of speech are coming under direct attack by Islamic Jihad.

How should Europe have responded? How shall Europe respond?

In my view, every newspaper in Europe and the Americas should have re-published the so-called offensive cartoons in order to reinforce the notion that freedom must not succumb to violence, threats or intimidation. Unfortunately, just the opposite was the case, as freedom retreated with each apology.

But is it not reasonable to ask the question: *Why does an Islamized Europe threaten the United States?*

Europe is a major power. In land mass it is larger than the United States and its population outnumbers that of America. Europe, as a colony of Islamofascism, poses a grave threat to the security and survival of <u>our</u> culture. Virulent anti-American policies emanating from Europe or "Eurabia" would threaten our trade policies and our economy. Without Europe as a political partner, our ability to deal with the threat of a nuclear Iran is severely compromised. An Islamized Europe isolates the United States in its attempts to halt the spread of Islamofascism, as much as a pro-Communist Western Europe would have made it almost impossible to halt the spread of Communism during the Cold War. For example, 20 years after the fact, it is routinely acknowledged, perhaps begrudgingly by some, that the deployment of Pershing missiles to Western Europe by the United States in the 1980's upped the ante for Russia so much that the economic collapse of the USSR was hastened, accelerating the breakaway of the Eastern Block countries and the destruction of the Berlin Wall. The liberation of twenty million people, who for a generation lived under communist fascism, was the final result.

More importantly, an impotent Europe has *already* harmed us. The 9/11 attacks were plotted in Hamburg, Germany. The individual assassins of the leaders of Afghanistan's Northern Alliance (the opposition to the Taliban) all carried Belgian passports. Zacarias Moussaoui, just recently sentenced to life in prison in the United States for his part in the 9/11 attacks, was *born in France and educated in Britain.* More recently, the foiled attacks by Islamofascists in their attempts to blow up airliners en-route from England to the United States, was planned and almost carried out by Islamofascists based in England and continental Europe.

Economically speaking, as the U.S. does everything possible to work with the international community to rein-in Iran's nuclear ambitions, France is clearly not our ally. France finds itself in the position of being Iran's largest creditor nation, so it is conflicted in its loyalties. Germany shows up as the largest lender to the countries of Syria and North Korea. As a result, America's struggle becomes that much more difficult when even our old Cold War allies are aligned against the U.S. in order to protect their own economic self-interest.

## BUT WHAT ABOUT BRITAIN?

Unfortunately, Tony Blair and his unwavering support of the U.S. may be the last breath of comfort from even our oldest and culturally closest ally. Blair is in his last year of office. There are two influential segments of British society that hate the United

States, no less than if they had been educated in Mecca. These segments, Britain's traditionally leftist academics and trade unions on the one hand, and Britain's ever growing Muslim population on the other, are finding common ground in a common enemy, the U.S. This bodes ill for England's continuing support of United States' foreign policy. After the publication of the offensive cartoons that sparked Muslim riots worldwide, some of the most hateful demonstrations against the publications arose in England. Placards not shown to the American people by the mainstream media, that were being held by British citizens of Muslim descent, stated such confrontational slogans as, "Europe, your real holocaust is coming "

Britain's academics and intellectual crowd, like their counterparts in the United States (See Chapter 4) share the same anti-all-things-American sentiment. Unfortunately, this anti-Americanism is a much more virulent strain than that found in the United States. Note the words of British playwright, Harold Pinter (winner of the Nobel Prize for literature, no less) in 2002, *before* America's invasion of Iraq: "The U.S. administration is now a bloodthirsty wild animal. Bombs are its only vocabulary." [xxi] Thank goodness America's "vocabulary" spoke loud and clear: the leader of Al-Qaeda in Iraq, Al-Zachari, is no longer around to behead American journalists on TV, or anyone else who might disagree with his utopian vision of Muslim freedom and prosperity. In 2003 an opinion piece by Mr. Pinter appeared in London's

*Daily Telegraph* entitled, not so subtly, "*I Loathe America.*" The op-ed piece began with "My Anti-Americanism has become almost uncontrollable..."[xxii]
The re-election of George W. Bush in 2004 sent those folks over the edge. The anti-American hate is now filtering into the orations of highly elected British public officials as they sense from where the new direction of the political winds are blowing. Only one month after the British train and bus bombings of 2005, British MP George Galloway said this:

> "It's not the Muslims who are terrorists. The biggest terrorists are Bush and Blair... but it is definitely not a clash of civilizations. Bush doesn't have any civilization."[xxiii]

Does this awful rhetoric, even if "inartful," have an effect on the British populace? You bet it does. A February, 2003 poll commissioned by Britain's TV Channel 4 revealed that a majority of Britons view the U.S., *not Iraq*, as the bigger threat to world peace.[xxiv] The British Teachers Union followed suit, passing resolutions condemning the United States and its foreign policy. When you consider this information in conjunction with the fact that more people in Britain attend weekly services at mosques than worship at the Church of England, you begin to get the picture.

Is it too late? Has England forgotten the failure of Neville Chamberlain's appeasement policy? Winston Churchill, where are you?

And so, in the judgment of this average American citizen, it comes down to this: Europe, meaning its Caucasian people, has lost sense of its cultural and historical past. The European people have lost their present identity and therefore, and most importantly, they have lost their vision for the future. A people without vision will perish. For a generation, academic elites in both Europe and the United States have denigrated Western culture and its values. Without a sense of the past, why look to the future? As a result, Islam has marched into that spiritual and cultural vacuum. What happens after that? Those tolerant of the intolerant will perish.

Is it too late for Europe? Read the re-telling of the childhood fairytale, "The Three Little Pigs." This updated version could be re-titled "The Three Euro Pigs."

## THE THREE LITTLE PIGS

*In a form of prose meant for the youngest of readers*
Once upon a time there lived three little pigs. They lived alone in a great big beautiful old house. And inside the house of the three little pigs there were many beautiful pieces of art, sculpture and great works of literature.

Little pigs had been living in this great, big, beautiful old house for many, many years. Over the years, stories had been passed down from generation to generation about the big bad wolf. The story was repeated from grandpig to little pig that many, many years ago, the big bad wolf had come to huff and puff and blow the house down. As the old story was told, the big bad wolf would come to the door and yell: "Open the door and let me in, or I'll huff and I'll puff, and I'll blow your house in!" And the little pigs were always taught to say "no, no, no, not by the hair of our chinny, chin, chins." This was so because little pigs were always told that there were <u>differences</u> between pigs and wolves. The main difference between the two was that the big bad wolf liked to eat little pigs, even though pigs would never purposefully harm a wolf.

But, things had changed of late. When the three little pigs were younger and went to school, they were told that the big bad wolf really wasn't so bad. They were told that the only reason the big bad wolf ate little pigs was because in the past, many, many years ago, little pigs had been mean to the big bad wolf and killed wolves. The three little pigs were now being told that because the wolf hadn't eaten pigs in a long time, there was no longer a reason to fear the big bad wolf. And the three little pigs were told, both in schools and in everything they read, that there was really no difference between pigs and wolves. The three little pigs were told that the wolf culture was just as good as the pig culture. Even though the wolf culture had never invented the car, or the steam engine, or the train, or the airplane, or the printing press, or discovered cures to many diseases that formerly killed pigs for thousands of years; or even though the wolf culture had no art, music or literature that people everywhere appreciated, they were told that the wolf culture was just as good, if not better than the pig culture.

In fact, the three little pigs were now taught that the wolf should not be called the "big bad" wolf anymore. They were taught that calling the wolf the "big bad" wolf was intolerant and insensitive to the wolf's feelings. They were told that the "big bad" wolf was a stereotype developed back in the day when pigs were intolerant and insensitive. The pigs were now taught in school that they should be sensitive to other creatures so all creatures could live in harmony. And so, the story of the "big bad" wolf no longer scared the three little pigs. In fact, in many places the story was no longer even told, for fear of offending the wolves.

And then one day the three little pigs looked around and noticed that they had a number of empty and unoccupied bedrooms in their big, old, beautiful house. It seems that the three little pigs had been taught how to give pleasure to one another without having to worry about a lot of little baby pigs showing up as a result. And so, there were lots of empty bedrooms in the big old beautiful house.

And then one day, Mr. and Mrs. Wolf actually came to the door. But they didn't say "Open up, open up and let us in, or we'll huff and we'll puff and we'll blow your house in!" No, they said, "If you let us into your house, we promise that we'll cook for you and clean for you and do all the chores around the house that you don't want to do, and since you have all those extra rooms, we'll sleep there and we won't be any inconvenience at all." And because the old story of the big bad wolf had been forgotten, or dismissed as intolerant, the three little pigs thought this was a wonderful idea. They gladly opened the door to Mr. and Mrs. Wolf and they let Mr. and Mrs. Wolf into their house to live with them.

And after a while, the three little pigs noticed that Mr. and Mrs. Wolf had lots of little wolves running around their house. And Mr. and Mrs. Wolf said, "You still have lots of empty bedrooms in your house, so now that we have little wolves, can we use some more of your empty bedrooms?" And the little pigs agreed and soon the big old house was all filled up with the three little pigs, Mr. and Mrs. Wolf and lots of little wolves.

And then one day, a strange thing happened. George Pig, Jr. came by the house and stood on the sidewalk. George Pig, Jr. was the caretaker of the largest house in the whole neighborhood. In fact, to the three little pigs, they thought his house was a mansion. George Pig, Jr.'s house was on the other side of the pond, but it was plain for all to see that no other house could compare to it.

But on this day, George Pig, Jr. was visibly agitated. He told the three little pigs that some big bad wolves had driven a truck filled with dynamite into his house and lots of his fellow pigs were killed.

He said he knew which big bad wolves had done it and he was going to make sure it didn't happen again. So he was going over to the other side of the tracks, where the big bad wolves lived, and he was going to kill any wolf that was involved with that truck, including any wolf that owned the garage where the truck was parked before it drove over to his house and exploded.

George Pig, Jr. also said he knew about other wolves who were driving cars filled with dynamite into other pig houses in other neighborhoods. He said these big bad wolves were killing not only pigs, but other wolves, too. G.P., Jr. said he was going to kill them, too, so this whole business of driving cars and trucks into piggy houses and exploding them would stop. He added, " Sometimes pigs in smaller houses aren't strong enough to fight the big bad wolves all by themselves. But the little pigs in his house *were* strong enough, so he would help the other pigs. In this way the big bad wolves would not huff and puff any-more."

So G.P., Jr. said to the three little pigs, "I came by, because you live in a nice, big, old house and because you have been our friends for a long time, to see if you would help?"

For a minute, the three little pigs felt a rush of energy, for they had vague memories that at one time their parents were really good friends with the little pigs who lived in the big house across the pond, long before George Pig Jr. was the Caretaker.

But then they hesitated. They felt the presence of many wolf-eyes looking at them from behind. The wolves had listened to the whole conversation. The wolves' star-ing, unblinking eyes, and their presence in their home gave the three little pigs an uneasy feeling that they couldn't really describe.

Then they heard the breathing of the wolves behind them and the three little pigs huddled amongst themselves.

After some quiet discussion, the three little pigs said, "No thanks, George Pig, Jr. You are overreacting. You are a wild cowboy. Get help from somewhere else, we weren't the ones attacked."

G.P., Jr. listened, and though a bit bothered, continued on. He thought the three little pigs were underestimating the danger, but in his zeal to protect his own pigs, he was determined not to ignore the danger.

A number of years went by. G.P., Jr. got into a pretty good fight on the other side of the tracks, but that is another story.

Now, during this time of the big fight across the tracks, the baby wolves inside the big, old, nice house of the three little pigs became teenage wolves. And one day they looked around and saw all the nice things the three little pigs had, and how <u>they</u> had <u>no</u> nice things. And the teenage wolves said amongst themselves, "Many of us were born in this house, yet the three little pigs have all the nice things and we have none. That's not fair!"

So the teenage wolves went on a rampage. The young wolves wrecked a lot of things. But after a while the older wolves who first moved into the house got them to quiet down. You see, wolves are smart. They looked around and saw there were no teenage little pigs, and the three little pigs were getting old. So they kept still, knowing they could bide their time.

And during those years, there were other changes…

The wolves were <u>always</u> looking across the pond to the big old mansion on the other side. On past nights, they had seen the well-lit house alive with people. They could hear music, laughter and dancing...The wolves thought of their own situation and seethed with rage.

But lately, things began to change. They could hear shouting and fighting inside the mansion across the pond. They sometimes heard yelling that G.P., Jr., the Caretaker, was being unfair to the big, bad wolves and that he was a bad Caretaker. There was shouting that the wolves should be left alone. And the wolves listened and smiled with approval.

Now, after the young wolves went on a rampage the three little pigs all got together and decided that the wolves must be upset about their situation. So the three little pigs convened a meeting with the wolves.

The wolves demanded more of the things around the house <u>they</u> were used to. The wolves claimed the three little pigs were intolerant and insensitive to the plight of the wolves. The wolves complained that, in the past, the grandparents of the three little pigs had oppressed the wolves; so they wanted special consideration to make up for the past injustices. Many academic pigs agreed. So, over time, art, language,...and even the laws governing how the pig house would be run, began to change.

And then one day, the three little pigs just disappeared. No one knows if they left to go across the pond, or if they died, or if they were hiding in the basement.

But it wasn't long after that when the wolves decided that the art, music, literature and churches that were in the big old house when the wolves first moved in reminded them of <u>pigs</u> and not wolves. So, slowly over the years, the steeples turned into domes, and nobody spoke the language of the three little pigs anymore.

And it wasn't long after that when the big bad wolves, much larger in number now, stronger and with a more aggressive attitude from that of their parent wolves, traveled across the pond and demanded of the Caretaker of the mansion, "Let us in, let us in, or we'll huff and we'll puff and we'll blow your house in!" And what did those who lived in the mansion say? Was it, "Not by the hair of our chinny, chin, chin"?

Or ….

Like the three Euro pigs…

Did they just <u>let</u> them in?

It was centuries ago when the European soothsayer, Nostradamus, predicted "The camel will drink blood from the Rhine River." Is his prediction closer to reality than we think?

# CHAPTER 3
# THEY ARE COMING FOR YOU NEXT!
# (Over 1,000 Years of Aggression!)

*(A RELIGION OF PEACE?)*

In Chapter 1, it was reported that the newly elected leader of Palestine, from the Hamas organization, openly declared their intention to destroy Israel, America and the West.

There are some who suggest that if America would be less supportive of Israel and more respectful of nations that have issues with Israel, this would improve our relations with these nations and thus improve the prospects for peace. To this average citizen, this theory of foreign policy will only lead to more aggression and more violence by those that seek to end our way of life.

My great-grandfather was a coal miner in southern Illinois. Miners learn there are warning signs that tell of impending cave-ins or releases of poisonous gas. Canaries that live in the mine shaft suffer the disaster long before the humans do. They will die from the gasses or fly out of the mine shaft warning the miners of impending doom.

Persecution of the Jews is the canary in the mine. For example, the persecution of the Jews in the 1930's in Nazi Germany was at first considered a "Jewish problem." But the persecutions did not stop there. Next in line to be singled out for death by the Nazi fascists were the learning disabled, then gypsies, then Catholics, and then the enslavement and destruction of the population of Germany's neighboring countries (by then deemed inferior as well). And so it is, and will be, with Islamofascists. Appeasement of that kind of hate will only bring more of it. The persecution of the Jew is more often than not a harbinger of worse things to come, if not firmly opposed.

But hate for the Jew, while a rallying point for Islamofascists, is only one of many groups singled out for extermination. In Afghanistan, recently (2006), the legal system meted out the death sentence for a man whose only crime was his conversion from Islam to Christianity. Islamic law, entitled the "Sharia," requires death for all apostasy (renunciation of Islam). After world pressure was brought to bear on Afghanistan's leaders, the apostate was declared insane and mentally incompetent. This was the only reason his death sentence was commuted. He escaped and now resides in Italy.[xxv] But world pressure did not alter the enforcement of the law, nor did it change the law which was used to impose the death penalty.

Islamic intolerance is no recent phenomenon, however. What follows is not intended to be an exhaustive or in-depth discussion of the topic presented. It is meant only to be a cursory analysis of historical facts to accomplish two things:

Alert the reader to the danger we and our children face (which is the main purpose of this entire treatise), and...

Encourage the reader to conduct his or her own research so as to be better equipped to interpret and respond to the unfolding of world events.

## ISLAMIC LAW AND ITS TREATMENT OF NON-MUSLIMS.

Scholars agree there is no concept of equality of rights or dignity for non-Muslims.[xxvi] Citizens are divided into three categories, (1) Muslims, (2) People of the Book, (3) Others. It is permitted under the Quran and under the Sharia to kill infidels. For People of the Book (Jews and Christians), according to Muslim jurists, the following ordinances must be enforced on Christians and Jews who reside among Muslims:

They are not allowed to build new churches, temples or synagogues. Construction of *any* church, temple or synagogue on the Arabian peninsula is prohibited. You will find no Christian churches there, least of all Jewish temples.

In Saudi Arabia, it is illegal to wear any outward sign of Christianity.

Muslims are permitted to demolish all non-Muslim houses of worship in any land they conquer.

Jews and Christians are not allowed to pray or read their sacred books out loud, either at home or in churches, lest Muslims hear their prayers and be offended.

Jews and Christians are not allowed to print their religious books or sell them in public places and in markets in Islamic countries.

Christians are not allowed to install a cross on their houses or churches because it is a symbol of infidelity.

Christians and Jews are not permitted to broadcast or display their ceremonial religious rituals on radio or television or to use the print or broadcast media to publish any picture of their religious ceremonies.

Christians and Jews are not allowed to congregate in the streets during their religious festivals.

Christians and Jews are not allowed to join the army.

There is a complete double standard going on here. In the tolerant West, Muslims are perfectly willing to use our tolerance and our laws respecting freedom of speech, freedom of assembly and freedom of the press to force our acceptance of them. But should they assume political control, the reverse will not be the case. Note for example the Muslim demands to abolish freedom of the press and speech when it comes to the publication or utterances of things deemed offensive to Muslims. Tolerance is cultural suicide when it is a one- way street. (See Chapter 6)

The West's response to the satirical cartoons which depicted Mohammad with a bomb for a turban was completely wrong. Most newspapers in western cities around the world and in the United States refused to publish the cartoons for fear of further reprisals and for fear of further offense to the Muslim community. This willingness to abdicate our freedoms, especially freedom of the press, will only lead to further repression of those freedoms so as not to "offend" our neighbors. Islamofascists will use our political correctness to their advantage. Before you realize it, if you want to put a cross on your front lawn during the Christmas season, it will be considered a hate crime because it would show lack of sensitivity to your Muslim neighbor who happens to live next door. (See Chapter 6)

## HISTORY OF ISLAMIC DESTRUCTION OF INFIDEL PEOPLES.

At the time of Mohammad's birth, Christianity geographically encompassed, outside of Europe, the entire ancient Roman province of Asia, extending across the Caucasus mountains to the Caspian Sea, Syria, including the Holy Land and a wide belt of North Africa, from Egypt, west to the Atlantic Ocean. Christians in the world numbered over thirty million by AD 311. Most of them lived not in Europe, but in Asia Minor and Africa. This geographical area was the home to such Christian fathers as Paul of Tarsus,

Augustine of Hippo, Polycarp of Smyrna, Turtullian of Carthage, Clement of Alexandria, John Chrysostom of Antioch, and Cyprian of Carthage. The Seven Churches of the Revelation were all in Asia Minor. Smyrna was the last of these, and kept her Christian light burning until 1922 when the Turks destroyed it, along with its Christian population. [xxvii]

## MUSLIM CONQUEST PRECEDING THE CRUSADES

It is necessary to suggest that history may have been re-written by Western apologists and Western academic elites. Most of us were taught that the Crusades were an example of Western imperialism. And while much of the Crusades involved wrongful slaughter of innocents, another reading of history reveals that the Crusades were not wars of aggression but that of Christendom striking back at Muslim aggression.

The waves of conquest arising from the Muslim religion took place long before the Crusaders ever showed up. In the Muslim invasion of Syria in 634, thousands of Christians were massacred. In Mesopotamia (modern day Iraq), between 635 and 642, monasteries were ransacked and the monks and villagers slain. Around this same time period, in Egypt, all Christians were put to the sword. In Armenia, the entire population of Euchaita was wiped out. Muslim invaders sacked and pillaged Cypress and then established their rule by a great massacre. In North Africa, Tripoli was pillaged in 643 by Amr who forced the Jews and Christians to hand over their women and children as slaves to the Arab army. Carthage was razed to the ground and most of its inhabitants killed. [xxviii] For the millions of Christians and Jews living in the Middle East in the 7$^{th}$ Century, with the advent of Islam, a long night descended on that region of the world. By the time of the First Crusade at the beginning of the second century, Muslims had succeeded in massacring and occupying by force of arms the entire geographical area of the early Christian Church. As the centuries passed, Muslim aggression continued. In Europe, the Muslims crossed the Pyrenees mountains out of Spain, promising to stable their horses in St. Peter's at Rome! They were defeated, however, by Charles Martell at Tours, 100 years after Mohammed's death.

Far from being wars of imperialist advancement, therefore, the Crusades were the <u>belated military responses</u> of Christian Europe to three centuries of Muslim aggression against Christian lands, the systemic mistreatment of the indigenous Christian population of those lands, and the harassment of Christian pilgrims. The post-modern myth, promoted by Islamic propagandists and supported by self-hating Westerners, notably in the academy, claims that peaceful Muslims native to the Holy Land were forced to take up arms in defense of European-Christian aggression. This myth takes 1092 AD as its starting point but conveniently ignores the preceding <u>centuries</u> when Muslims swept through the Byzantine Empire, conquering about two-thirds of the Christian world at that time. For the Crusades, the driving impulse was not that of conquest and aggression, but of <u>recovery and defense</u> of the Holy Land in liberation of the Christians who, in many places, still constituted a majority of the population. The Crusades were a <u>reaction</u> to what the Muslims had done. The primary difference was this: the Crusades' killings were <u>in disobedience</u> of their scripture. The Muslim killings were in <u>accordance</u> with their Scripture.

The Crusade victories, however, were but a temporary setback to Islamic expansion. Between 1200 and 1900, massacres in India at the hands of Islamists were greater in sheer numbers than all of the deaths of the Holocaust.[xxix] The reign and expansion of the Ottoman Empire reached its peak in the 1500's when it controlled Egypt, Syria, present day Iran and as far west as the gates of Vienna in central Europe.[xxx] The Ottoman rule continued until the dissolution of the Ottoman Empire at the end of World War I.

It is amazing that in this age of rampant victimology, the persecution of Christians by Muslims has become a taboo subject in Western higher education. The silence and the lies perpetrated by the Western academies of higher learning and the media elite continues to blind us concerning the murderous history of Muslim expansionism. As to <u>why</u> this might be the case, see Chapter 4.

## CHRISTIAN PERSECUTION TODAY

Today in Iran, Christian spiritual leaders are executed. In Lebanon, since 1975 <u>hundreds of thousands</u> of Christians have been massacred, displaced or exiled.[xxxi] In the Sudan, since the Islamic takeover in 1989, <u>one million</u>

Sudanese have been killed because of their Christian faith. In Syria, at one time there were one million Christians in residence there. Today it is a stronghold of Islamofascism. In Egypt, as a result of British colonization, there used to be <u>millions</u> of Christians there. Where are they today? In Indonesia, the Barrabas Fund reported at the end of 2000, 500,000 Christians had been internally displaced, 5,000 killed and 7,000 forcibly converted to Islam. [xxxii]

A close examination of Islamofascist terror over the centuries reveals great similarities with its twentieth century totalitarian counterparts: Nazism and Communism. And while the methods may have been different (i.e., the Nazis had their concentration camps and the Communists had their Gulags), the ideology remains the same. Islamofacism, Nazi fascism or Communism all have in common the lust for other people's lives and property, and the desire to exercise complete control over their subjects' lives. All three have been justified by a self-reverential system of thought and belief that perverts meanings of words, stunts our sense of moral clarity, and destroys souls.

William Muir was an esteemed historian of the Orient who lived between 1819 and 1905. At the end of a long and distinguished career of studying the Middle East, he declared his conviction:

> "The sword of Mohammad and the Quran
> are the most fatal enemies of civilization,
> liberty and truth which the world has yet
> known. They have combined to create an

unmitigated cultural disaster, parading as God's will." [xxxiii]

Consider the words of Winston Churchill a generation later:

> "How dreadful are the curses which Mohammedanism lays on its votaries. Besides the fanatical frenzy, which is as dangerous in a man as hydrophobia in a dog, there is this fearful fatalistic apathy… Individual Moslems may show splendid qualities, but the influence of the religion paralyzes the social development of those who follow it…. Far from being moribund, Mohammedanism is a militant and proselytizing faith. It has already spread throughout Central Africa, raising fearless warriors at every step; and were it not that Christianity is sheltered in the strong arms of science, the civilization of modern Europe might fall, as fell the civilization of ancient Rome." [xxxiv]

Note Churchill's reference to the saving grace of the "strong arms of science." This obviously refers to the West's technological superiority in weaponry and armaments since the late eighteenth through the twentieth century. Should Iran obtain nuclear weapons capability, or other weapons of mass destruction similar to what was believed to have been possessed by Saddam Hussein in Iraq, Churchill's concern that the civilization of modern Europe would go the way of ancient Rome could well come to pass.

When the Mufti of Jerusalem declared at the Dome of the Rock in Jerusalem in 2001, that negation of Jewish existence was an existential need of Islam, he was and is reflecting a majority, main street Middle East Muslim position, continuing a well established tradition of over a thousand years. [xxxv]

Wake up, America! Do not let unbridled immigration or our own apathy allow the sword of the prophet to destroy us. If "People of the Book," Jews and Christians, unite in their understanding of the threat they face and if we in the West have the moral courage to act, Judeo-Christianity will survive. (See Chapter 7) So why is the media not warning us or reporting to us more on this danger? That is the subject of Chapter 4…

# CHAPTER 4
# WHY THE NEWS MEDIA IS NOT TELLING US THE TRUTH ABOUT ISLAMOFASCISM

## (*THE ENEMY OF MY ENEMY IS MY FRIEND*)

The analysis for this chapter is presented in two parts. **Part 1** is a brief examination of the intellectual mindset of the academy and media elites today. **Part 2** is a story similar to the "Three Little Pigs" allegory of Chapter 2, but the animals are sheep, wolves and sheepdogs.

## PART 1
## THE UNSPOKEN ALLIANCE BETWEEN ISLAMOFASCISTS AND THE AMERICAN LEFT

The misreporting and unwillingness of the mainstream media to tell us the truth about the war against

Islamofascism begins with the premise that the mainstream media is leftist and overwhelmingly Democrat. As a result, the press and broadcast media are dually incentivized to misreport or negatively report the truth about the war on Islamofascism.

    A. The Premise: The mainstream media is very left, very Democrat and very out of touch with mainstream America.

        1. Who is the mainstream media?

           (a) The print media.

For the purposes of this discussion, the mainstream print media includes such newspapers as the *New York Times*, the *Los Angeles Times*, the *Atlanta Constitution*, the editorial boards of just about every American newspaper in the United States and weekly journals such as *Time* and *Newsweek*.

           (b) The broadcast media

For the purposes of this discussion, the mainstream broadcast media includes ABC, NBC, CBS, CNN and MSNBC.

The bias of the mainstream media has been extensively discussed. Initially, and most famously, by Bernard Goldberg in his 2002 book entitled <u>Bias</u>, subtitled "A CBS insider exposes how the media distorts the news." This became a *New York Times* bestseller. Bernard Goldberg was the first "insider" to reveal what most Americans had suspected for a long time. Goldberg writes, "...there isn't a well-orchestrated, vast left-wing conspiracy in America's newsrooms. The bitter truth...is ...worse." [xxxvi]

And here is the kicker: Goldberg was an <u>insider</u> for 28 years, so if anyone would know about liberal or leftist bias in the newsrooms, it would be him. Bernard Goldberg was a CBS news correspondent from 1972 until the summer of 2000. He knows the business and, as he wrote in his book, he knows what the news media does <u>not</u> want the public to see.

Here are some statistics from a survey conducted in 1996 by the Roper Center, a widely respected polling organization:

In 1992, <u>89</u>% of Washington, D.C. journalists voted for Bill Clinton. Yet only <u>43</u>% of the rest of the voting public chose Bill Clinton. <u>7</u>% of D.C. journalists voted for George Bush, Sr. in that same election even though <u>40</u>% of the rest of the country voted for him. Consider the 89% number that voted for Bill Clinton. Even the most disinterested observer of politics knows that <u>no</u> candidate wins by that kind of margin unless, of course, you are Fidel Castro or Saddam Hussein!

So if 9 out of 10 journalists in Washington voted for a President that failed to garner even one-half of the rest of the nation's vote, can the media that reports the news coming out of Washington, D.C. possibly be fair and balanced? The statistics get worse. Political polling shows that the U.S. is about evenly divided between Republicans and Democrats. However, can you guess what percentage of journalists identify themselves as Republicans? Four percent (4%) of those that bring you the news identified themselves as such! And when asked to characterize their political orientation, 61% said liberal and 9% said conservative or moderate to conservative! [xxxvii]

But this poll taken in the 1990's revealed nothing new. In 1972, a poll taken of the newsrooms showed that <u>70%</u> of the journalists voted for Democrat George McGovern for President. Yet in that election his opponent, Republican Richard Nixon carried every state in the Union except Massachusetts. That statistic bears repeating. Nixon beat McGovern in the popular vote in 49 states, yet over <u>two-thirds</u> of all journalists voted for Senator McGovern.

More recently, in March of 2000 the *Orlando Sun-Sentinel* conducted a poll of 3,400 journalists. The results were as follows:

The media are, as compared to the public-at-large:

Less likely to get married and have children.

Less likely to own homes.

Less likely to go to a church or synagogue.

How many of the journalists polled belonged to the American Legion or service organizations like the Rotary Club? Zero. [xxxviii]

There's more. Who said this? "I hope his wife feeds him lots of eggs and butter and he dies early, like many black men do, of heart disease." Was it a right-wing extremist? No, that terribly racist statement was uttered by a supposedly well respected *USA Today* columnist, Julianne Malveaux. She gets away with it because she was referring to a <u>conservative</u>. And who might that conservative have been? It was none other than United States Supreme Court Justice Clarence Thomas. [xxxix]

Want still more? *The Los Angeles Times* printed an op-ed piece by Karen Grigsby Bates who was writing about then Senate Majority Leader of the United States Senate, Trent Lott:

> "...whenever I hear Trent Lott speak, I immediately think of nooses decorating trees. Big trees, with black bodies swinging from the business end of the nooses." [xl]

However, when syndicated columnist George Will wrote in one of his columns, "I think it is reasonable to believe that (Bill Clinton) was a rapist," the *Los Angeles Times*, the same newspaper that allowed Karen Grigsby Bates to write, in essence, that Senate Majority Leader Trent Lott was a racist murderer, censored out of Will's article his comment about Bill Clinton. [xli]

What is the lesson here? Because of media bias, certain newspapers will allow to be printed a reference to a Republican Senate Majority Leader as a Ku-Klux-Klan murderer, but a reference to a Democrat President in a negative light gets put on the editor's cutting room floor. [xlii]

It becomes a rhetorical question as to whether bias in the media infects its coverage of the news, including the war on Islamofascism. For example, why doesn't the media ask hard questions of the Islamists as well? For instance, "In the five years of continued Muslim terrorist activity all over the world since 9/11, what exactly is in the Quran that justifies murder?" Or, "Why are there no Christian, Jewish or Hindu suicide (homicide) bombers?"[xliii] I suggest you won't see in-depth news shows covering such topics because such might cast Islam in a negative light.

Is there then, what others have characterized as, an "unholy alliance" between the American left, a pseudonym for the media, and Islamofascism? The answer is yes. The word "alliance" suggests a knowing, but perhaps unspoken affinity between the two groups, the Islamofascists and the American left.

The "alliance" has everything to do with both their dislike for America and capitalism but little to do, necessarily, with the left's agreement with the ideology of the Islamofascists. Hence, "The enemy of my enemy is my friend." This antipathy by the left of all things American actually goes back generations and was imported from Europe. The importation of this radicalism and instruction of anti-Americanism continues today.

Those that educate our children in our colleges and universities today came of age in the 60's during the height of the Vietnam War. In that time, they in turn were taught by academics who were in colleges and universities in the 30's, during the Great Depression. It was in this hard-scrabble environment that the socialist, anti-capitalist movement was at its peak in Europe and America.

Herbert Aptheker wrote and taught in American academic institutions in the 40's, 50's, 60's, 70's and 80's. His book *History and Reality*, first published in

1949, became a foundational book for leftist historians that emerged after the Vietnam War. Therein, Aptheker wrote:

> "The global capitalist system is so putrid...that it no longer dares permit the people to live at all...The American ruling class have the morals of goats, the learning of gorillas, and the ethics of... racist, war inciting, enemies of humanity, rotten to the core, parasitic, merciless and doomed." [xliv]

Aptheker's venom might be dismissed if he had become irrelevant or had adjusted his belief system after the collapse of Communism and the end of the Cold War.

Unbelievably, oblivious to the reality of real-world events, as Communist governments and state-run economies collapsed in country after country, and unmoved by America's technological advances and phenomenal rise in its standard of living in the 80's and 90's, Aptheker remained an unrepentant Communist and an unabashed hater of all things American. He became the role model for the next generation of radicals and college professors.

In a sequence of events that would appall the average American, but was perfectly acceptable in academic circles, at the end of his career in the 1990's, Aptheker was given an appointment as a visiting professor at Bryn Mawr University and an appointment to one of the University of California's most prestigious law schools. Before his death in 2003, he was formally honored as a scholar by the History Department of Columbia University.[xlv] Aptheker was in his prime in the late 60's and his student disciples <u>now</u> rule the Academy.

This writer went to college in the 1970's, specifically 1971 through 1975. I was a political science major in a small, elite northeastern college. I took "Marxism," but "Capitalism" was never offered as a course of study. Personally, I obtained an "A" in Marxism because I learned how to regurgitate pro-Marxist, anti-capitalist dogma. If I had followed that rule in all of my other classes, I might have graduated <u>summa cum laude</u>! I never believed any of that stuff, but there were plenty of students that did. And now <u>those</u> students are in their fifties and find themselves as department chairmen and chairwomen of colleges and universities across America. They occupy positions of influence on editorial boards of newspapers and T.V. stations throughout the country.

So today we are witnessing the 60's generation of the Vietnam war protesters coming of age, many of which now occupy positions of authority, power and influence everywhere. Their mind-set can be summed up as follows: Because America is an unjust society, all of its wars are unjust. Period. Therefore, America's reasons for entering Afghanistan or Iraq are tainted <u>before</u> the fact. The fact that no weapons of mass destruction were found in Iraq only adds to their view of the war as immoral.

Recall some of the media's comments before the invasion of Afghanistan. Do you remember that it was going to be a quagmire, a land war in Asia and like the Russians before, the excursion was doomed to failure?

Some of the leading liberal institutions of higher learning in the United States today, which one might even characterize as anti-mainstream American, are Yale University (with the Taliban leader as a student), Columbia University, Brown University, Cornell University, the University of California at Berkeley, Bryn Mawr, the University of California at Los Angeles, the University of California at Davis, The City University of New York, Harvard University, Princeton University, Vassar College, NYU, and the University of South Florida. Does this list of the "prestigious" universities surprise you? It should not. Their lack of connectivity with the average American is the dirty little secret that allows alumni dollars to keep flowing back to those campuses. These are many of the feeder schools for American journalists that comprise our press corps and editorial boards today.

But the Left failed at the election game. Since the 1980's, the electorate has become Republican. The Left has also failed to capture the attention of working class American families. This, in and of itself, shows the Left's lack of understanding of democratic capitalism. In America there is no permanent working class. America's unprecedented upward mobility of its people breaks the old Marxist stereotype of the "working class." As a result, the Left has turned to and has unfortunately succeeded in capturing the heart and soul of America's colleges and universities.

How many people remember the S.D.S.? (Students For a Democratic Society) I do because I was there. In 1969 in downtown New Haven, Connecticut, home to Yale University, I watched as the S.D.S. literally started a riot. People got hurt, tear gassed and there was shooting. It was the ugliest thing I ever saw. The "Doors" wrote a song about it called "Peace Frog." One of the lines from that song was "Blood in the streets in the town of New Haven." The S.D.S. were violent, angry and anarchists.

One of its leaders, Todd Gitlin, is now a Professor of Sociology and Journalism at Columbia University. He summed up the Left's academic triumph in the academy as follows:

> "My generation of the new Left—a generation that grew as the Vietnam War went on—relinquished any title to patriotism without much sense of loss...All that was left to the Left was to unearth righteous traditions and cultivate them in universities. The much mocked "political correctness" of the next academic generation was a <u>consolation</u> prize. We lost—we squandered—the politics, <u>but we won in the textbooks</u>."[xlvi]

Well renowned schools such as Harvard, Yale and UNC (University of North Carolina) offer courses such as

"Whiteness Studies," "Cultural Studies," "Women's Studies," "African American Studies," and "American Studies." In many cases, those courses and their names are euphemisms for a curriculum that is devoted to nothing less than a radical assault on American history and traditional American values.

Even law schools have been subverted by this political ideology. Consider the following passage from a legal text at an institution generally known as a very good law school—Georgetown. The legal text concerns the 14th Amendment which applies our Bill of Rights to state laws, guaranteeing the Bill of Rights freedoms for all citizens. The text states:

> "The political history of the United States that culminated and is reflected in the Constitution, is in large measure a history of almost unthinkable brutality towards slaves, genocidal hatred of Native Americans, racist devaluation of non-whites, and sexist devaluation of women..."[xlvii]

Please allow a slight digression. This selective view of history fundamentally distorts America's influence on social mores and America's great heritage. Two hundred years ago, America was the first country in the world to reject a monarchy, throw off colonialism and declare all these "[t]ruths as self-evident. All men are created equal." (under the law)

This was revolutionary! Seventy-five years later, America literally tore itself apart in a civil war to end slavery. Fifty years later, America led another world-wide revolution by giving women the right to vote. The equality of women in the voting booth represented a huge step forward in women's rights, again leading the world in this regard. Over the next ninety years, Americans, by force of arms, force of will, and force of ideas, liberated <u>millions</u> from totalitarian tyrannies around the world.

America's medical technology has healed and cured millions from diseases that have plagued mankind since the dawn of creation. America's economic order has provided more prosperity and more hope for more people than any society in the history of the world. The average citizen should be told, and our students must be so educated so that the radicals in our media and universities can be opposed. We must reclaim our heritage, reclaim our identity as a nation, and reclaim the vision of America. What is that vision? That America continues to be a city on a hill, a light to the world, and a beacon of hope for oppressed people everywhere.

---

Although this has not been an exhaustive analysis of the bias in the academy and the media, what you read here is not an aberration but mainstream in the academy. We average folks must filter everything we see and hear through the prism of the academy, being aware of the environment of indoctrination from which our news reporters have been birthed.

## HOW DOES THIS AFFECT THE WAY THE WAR ON ISLAMOFASCISM IS REPORTED?

The most obvious manifestation of this bias is the hatred of all things Republican, and especially Bush. This is especially so when there are many journalists who still believe that George W. Bush is an illegitimate President as a result of the 2000 election.

Thus, many in the media are loathe to report <u>anything</u> that might reflect positively on the Bush administration or its foreign policy decisions. The mainstream media will only begrudgingly give the Bush Administration credit for things gone right, but will pick up immediately on their coverage of any event that shows things gone wrong. But this book is not an apology for the Bush Administration. It too has failed in properly informing the average American (us) about the threat we face.

But returning to the bias in the media, the coverage of the so-called prison abuse scandal is a perfect example. The media reporting of Senator Durbin's remarks (the Senior Senator from Illinois) comparing the Bush Administration to the Nazi reign in Germany was actually portrayed as a serious comment. Take note, the so-called "abuse" of prisoners at Guantanamo was less than what many endured at their college fraternity initiation in their freshman year of college.

How Muslim prisoners were being treated at Guantanamo was never compared and contrasted to the <u>beheading</u> of reporter Daniel Pearl. American missteps, minor by comparison to human rights violations of other governments, are always examined in a vacuum of other human events. Islam gets a pass while we in the West are held to an arbitrary standard that is impossible to live up to. The United Nations sounds a call to close Guantanamo, where prisoners are given the Quran but the bible is not allowed so as not to offend the Muslims. The UN denounces America for its perceived human rights abuses while it barely acknowledges ethnic cleansing against Christians in the Sudan and gross abuses of human rights in Iran and other Muslim countries around the world.

Unfortunately, the negative coverage and media bias runs much deeper than the simple fact that a Republican occupies the White House. The hatred of all things Western has been the prevailing intellectual dogma spewed by colleges and universities throughout the country for over a generation. This anti-mainstream American dogma has been inculcated into the minds and in some cases, the hearts of students for 40 years. Somehow, the cold judgment of history evidenced by the decline and fall of Communism and other freedom-hating regimes has not mattered. Sean Hannity calls them the "blame America first" crowd. The sense of the American ideal has been lost. Unabashed American patriotism is ridiculed. Who America is, its national identity and its role in world history is no longer taught in a positive fashion.

Emerging from this intellectual incubator, many journalists today have no feel for the soul of America. They have no understanding of, as Alexis de Toqueville wrote almost 200 years ago in "Democracy in America," the fundamental goodness of America's people.[xlviii] As a result, there is <u>zero</u> chance that the mainstream press can be "fair and balanced." The American people instinctively sense this, which accounts for the overwhelming popularity of Fox News, which in turn only infuriates the mainstream media all the more.

Is there an answer? Yes.

---

## PART 2
## THE SHEEP, THE WOLF AND THE SHEEPDOG [xlix]

I'll conclude this chapter with a story of the sheep, the wolf and the sheepdog.

Once upon a time there was this big old ranch. This giant plot of land was called the "Big Earth Ranch." It was populated by many different creatures. But the Big Earth Ranch was run by only the most intelligent of the creatures: talking wolves, talking sheep and talking sheepdogs.

All three of the superior creatures were basically equal in intelligence. The difference between them was only in how they treated one another.

Sheep were kind, decent animals not capable of hurting one another or wolves, or sheepdogs, unless by accident or unless under <u>extreme</u> provocation. In fact, if the Big Earth Ranch was populated by only sheep, well, the Ranch would be very peaceful. Unfortunately, Big Earth Ranch had other intelligent creatures called wolves, and they were nothing like sheep. They especially liked to feed on the most defenseless of creatures, including sheep.

Now, there was a lot of debate as to why there

were even wolves at all or why wolves acted the way they did. Most sheep preferred to go on about their business, ignoring the fact that wolves existed or even denying that they existed altogether.

Sheep understood there were dangers in the Big Earth Ranch, like fire and bad weather. So they supported fire alarms, firefighters and weathermen. But sheep could not handle the fact that there were other talking creatures that roamed the Big Earth Ranch that wished to harm them. Sheep were inflicted with the inherent inability to see other creatures on the Ranch for what they really were. They could only see them as sheep: peaceful and non-violent.

That is why there were sheepdogs. If it weren't for sheepdogs, sheep would have become extinct many generations ago. Sheepdogs were <u>born</u> to protect and defend sheep. They <u>lived</u> to confront the wolf.

Here was the problem. Most sheep didn't like sheepdogs. The sheepdog was a reminder that there were wolves on the Big Earth Ranch and sheep didn't like to admit that. They also didn't like the sheepdog because in order to protect the sheep, the sheepdog looked and acted a lot like a wolf and that made sheep uncomfortable. The sheep liked to pretend that the wolf didn't even exist or even fantasized that wolves and sheep could get along if they just talked things out.

But when the wolf did show up ready to eat, the sheep would always rediscover how much they appreciated the sheepdog. The sheep from France were most like that. French sheep would say all kinds of bad things about the sheepdog until the wolf marched through Paris. Then the sheepdog became a hero. But then the danger passes, and the sheepdog becomes unpopular again.

Now inside the Big Earth Ranch there was the American Ranch, one of the largest spreads inside the Big Earth Ranch.

On September 11, 2001, the wolves showed up inside the American Ranch. On that day the wolves killed a bunch of sheep. Sheepdogs became very popular for a while. Later, however, the sheep began complaining about the sheepdogs. Sheep have short memories. The wolves count on that. In the Europe Ranch, the sheep were in charge. The sheep of the Europe Ranch were willing to risk their lives and their entire Ranch on the proposition that sheep and wolves could live harmoniously together, forgetting or rewriting memories and history. But the American Ranch was different.

It was founded by sheepdogs and was always a nation filled with sheepdogs. There were professional sheepdogs, amateur sheepdogs, mommy sheepdogs, daddy sheepdogs, and sheepdogs who, for generations, were imbued with an attitude within that said, "If it's going to be, it's up to me." If his neighbor's house got blown away, he wouldn't wait for FEMA to show up to get help. He would get with other sheepdogs and… just get it done. Afterward, without fanfare, the sheepdog would go back to his own life. There were sheepdogs on United Flight 93 and the mission of that homicide flight was defeated.

But over on the Europe Ranch, some time later, a terrible thing happened. The sheep disappeared. Some sheep got eaten by the wolves. Some sheep stopped having lambs and died off. Many sheepdogs on the Europe Ranch didn't like how the sheep treated them, so they went over to the American Ranch where they were appreciated. Plus, there weren't that many sheep left on the Europe Ranch to protect. That's when the Europe Ranch became filled with wolves and it became a very violent, unhappy place.

And then all the children wanted to know what happened to the American Ranch? That is the last chapter of the fairytale and it is being written now. So, go thank an American sheepdog, while you still can, and maybe the story will have a happy ending.

My belief... my hope, is that America is <u>still</u> a nation of sheepdogs. Ultimately, that is the answer.

## CHAPTER 5
# THE ENEMY WITHIN:
## Islamofascists in the U.S. and Their Unwitting Collaborators

*"We have met the enemy and he is us."*

—-*Pogo*

### 1. MOSQUES

America has a long history of non-governmental interference with the practice of religions. Traditionally, religious and clerical institutions have not only been left alone by our government, but encouraged (through taxation policies), because it has been generally accepted, and rightly so, that such religious institutions, arising primarily out of the Judeo-Christian tradition, were and are forces for good. Hospitals, orphanages, shelters, soup kitchens and thousands of other such charitable endeavors have provided food, clothing, shelter and spiritual sustenance to millions. Private charitable giving, either through foundations or individuals, exceeds that of all other countries. I dare say the United States' citizenry has been the greatest private charitable giver in the history of civilization. Unfortunately, with the rise of radical Islam, the concept that some religious institutions are a force for good within the United States must be re-examined.

Many Imams throughout the world have been trained in Saudi Arabia, and the largest university for the training of imams, the Saudi Kingdom, is Imam Mohammad ibn Saud Islamic University, located in Riyadh. The school is the largest Wahabbi university in the world. Of importance to all Americans is the fact that at least two, and maybe as many as nine of the university's graduates were 9/11 hijackers. In January of 2004, the State Department revoked the diplomatic visas of 16 people affiliated with the university's branch in Fairfax, Virginia because it was "promoting a brand of Islam that is intolerant of Christianity, Judaism and other religions." Unfortunately, intolerance of Christianity and Judaism and violence against infidels is preached weekly in mosques across the United States. In an interview conducted on January 22, 2007 with Joe Kaufman (a frequent columnist for *FrontPageMag.com,* Joe founded Americans Against Hate and CAIRWatch and has spent the last five years researching terrorism in the United States), in response to the question, "Do you believe that there are mosques within the United States that are fronts for terrorist organizations?" Joe responds

> "The vast majority of the mosques in the southeast United States are havens for radical Islam because of the circumstances under which they came about. The individuals that lead these mosques, the Board members that lead these mosques, the radical speakers that they have that pass through each of these mosques, and the organizations that created the mosques in the first place, all of these lend towards radical behavior that could possibly result in a terrorist attack."

In response to a question as to whether radical Islam within the United States is currently a threat to the peace and security of U.S. citizens, Joe says:

> "Oh, yes, with the number of mosques that are going up year after year after 9/11, there is a definite threat inside the U.S. and it's only growing, it's not lessening, because the United States refuses to take action against any of the mosques, including the ones that have been involved with Al-Qaeda, that have been involved with the 1993 bombing of the World Trade Center or 9/11. So

until the United States starts to crack down and maybe shut some of these places down, they're just going to be popping up over and over again."[1]

More concretely, in reviewing recent cases brought against Islamic terrorist cells within the United States, one commonality appears: the connection between the terrorist cell's members and a local mosque. The six men of the Al-Qaeda sleeper cell in Lackawanna, New York, arrested by the F.B.I. in 2001 for attending an Al-Qaeda terrorist training camp in Afghanistan, all belonged to the same Lackawanna mosque. One of the six arrested, Sahim Alwan, was the former president of the Lackawanna Islamic mosque. The six men grew up in the Yemeni community within Lackawanna. They were recruited by Kamal Derwish, a Yemeni American who was teaching about Islam in the Lackawanna Islamic mosque.

On the West Coast, a Sunni mosque in suburban Beaverton, Oregon was the meeting ground for six members indicted by federal authorities in 2002 for conspiring to provide aid to the Taliban and Al-Qaeda terrorists. F.B.I. documents allege the Imam of the mosque, Sheik Mohamed Abdirahman Kariye, used $12,000 collected from the members of the mosque to fund the efforts of the "Portland Six" to join the Taliban. A second Oregon mosque, also in Beaverton, collected thousands of dollars from its worshipers by claiming that the money was needed to help the parents of two members of the mosque in Saudi Arabia.

In reality it was to finance their trip to join the Taliban.[li]

The Al-Farooq mosque in Brooklyn has been in the public spotlight for more than 10 years as a hotbed of Islamic radicalism, sedition and treason. The Imam there, Sheik Omar Abdel-Rahman, was convicted in 1995 of conspiracy to bomb New York City landmarks. The Al-Farooq mosque collected money that was personally delivered to Osama bin Laden.[lii] Abdel-Rahman was also a regular speaker at the Al-Salaam mosque in Jersey City, New Jersey where many of the suspects in the 1993 World Trade Center bombing regularly worshipped.

In 2003, Amin Awad, a Muslim chaplain who counsels inmates in New York's Ryker's Island jail, was reassigned because of his links to terrorist fundraising. Just before his reassignment, Awad was named President of the Board of Trustees at the Al-Farooq mosque.

American mosques are regular stops on fundraising trips for terrorist leaders and their sympathizers. Osama bin Laden's chief deputy, Ayman Al-Zawahiri, made at least two money-raising trips to the United States in the 1990's, collecting money at the various mosques along the way. Prominently featured were mosques in Santa Clara, Stockton, and Sacramento, California.

Mosques in the United States are no different than mosques across the world. Militant Islam operates in mosques everywhere as their central meeting place. In reviewing the movie, "Obsession: Radical Islam's

War Against the West," Imams are quoted throughout the Middle East preaching their special brand of hate, violence and murder against Israel, the United States and all infidels. It is no accident that most U.S. mosques have become appendages of this worldwide Jihad against the West. The number of Muslims emigrating to the United States has been rising rapidly within the last 20 years. At the end of World War II, there were about 50 mosques located in the United States. Today there are over 1,300, and the number grows monthly. But building mosques costs money. Where does that money come from?

## 2. MONEY
Primarily, the money comes from all of us. What? The money is generated by the sale of oil, and oil is refined to create gasoline—gasoline that powers Western civilization. In effect, one could argue we are financing the very terrorists that seek to destroy us.

The Saudis built more than 60% of the mosques constructed in the 1980's and 1990's. According to one estimate, by 2002 the Saudis had spent more than $70 billion to fund 80% of the mosques built in the United States in the last 20 years.[liii] One of those mosques, the Bilal Islamic Center in Los Angeles, California, was one of the addresses given by Mark Fidel Kools, also known as Asan Akbar, the 101st Airborne sergeant who killed a fellow serviceman and wounded 15 others with a grenade in Kuwait shortly after the Iraq war began in March, 2003.

And if Saudi money is not available, in the case of

Sh'ia mosques, Iranian funds are there to step into the vacuum. Unfortunately, the mainstream media is again reluctant to do the investigative work required to establish that mosques are being used as recruiting grounds or sanctuaries for terrorists. As a result, Americans by and large continue to go uninformed, completely unaware that the mosque a block from the corner convenience store could this very night be planning the next bomb attack.

## 3. FRONTS

CAIR (Council on American Islamic Relations): According to Joe Kaufman and others, CAIR has raised money for terrorist charities prior to 9/11 and fortunately, since 9/11, some of those charities have been shut down. They've had four individuals that have been charged with terrorist activity. Two were deported and two were convicted. One national board member of CAIR was listed in the United States Attorneys' list of potential co-conspirators in the 1993 bombing of the World Trade Center. Even our government is being completely fooled in the sense that CAIR, of all organizations, actually conducts sensitivity training for the F.B.I.!

The Muslim Student Association, an innocuous sounding name, also supports and funds radical Islam in the United States. Radical Islam well understands America's brand of "political correctness" and the tolerance of "free speech" in academic circles. Radical Islam well knows that, in the name of toler-ance, universities and educational establishments will turn a blind eye in the name of "academic freedom" to any radical Islamist propagandizing or teaching seditious activities. The Islamic holy war in America, which is currently being funded and fomented in our universities across the United States under the banner of "academic freedom," is America's Trojan Horse; it is the elephant in the room that nobody wants to recognize; it is the emperor who has no clothes, that no one wants to acknowledge.

Anti-American rhetoric from Islamic professors, Imams and Muslim leaders is ignored. Sedition is not protected free speech. Islamic university professors are supported by their non-Muslim colleagues who belong to the "blame America first" crowd in world affairs. Columbia University professor of anthropology and Latin America studies, Nicholas DeGenova, said, "U.S. flags are the emblem of the invading war machine in Iraq today. They are the emblem of the occupying power. The only true heroes are those who find ways that help defeat the U.S. military."[liv] The American university has become the perfect place for militant Islam to hide.

Islamic charities also act as fronts for the collection and distribution of American dollars to teach radical Islam and foment sedition. The Islamic Association for Palestine (IAP) is a Hamas front. Yet, its leader, Abu Marzook, was welcomed at the Clinton White House and had top-level briefings there.[lv] Prior to that, tax records show that Abu Marzook donated a cash payment of $210,000 to the Holy Land Foundation for Relief and Development. A raid on a Hamas center in 1992 in Jenine, Israel uncovered a cache of Holy Land Foundation documents identifying the organization as an arm of Al-Qaeda.

However, the Bush administration can be faulted as well. In addition to CAIR providing sensitivity training to F.B.I. agents, I have been told confidentially that Karen Hughes, a close Bush ally, lobbies for the Muslim cause wherever possible.[lvi] As far as I am aware, President Bush, in the 5½ years since 9/11, has used the term "Islamic fascism" one time, on the fifth anniversary of those deadly attacks. After criticism by Muslim groups in the United States, no reference has been made since concerning the radical Muslim ideology of hate, death and violence that continues to be spread, not only around the world, but right here in the United States. (For a more detailed analysis of the secret Islamic terrorist networks within the United States, consult *Holy War on the Home Front*, by Harvey Kushner, published by the Penguin Group, 2004.)

## 4. PRISONS

Chuck Colson first gained fame (or infamy) when he was Special Counsel to the President of the United States and was sentenced to prison for his obstruction of justice and other crimes arising out of the Watergate activities under the Nixon administration. Following his prison experience, Chuck Colson founded a non-profit organization entitled, "Prison Fellowship," and has dedicated the past 20 years of his life to spreading the Gospel of Jesus Christ inside our prison system (wherever and whenever the prison authorities will allow, which in many states is restricted).

Colson's experiences in the prison system within the last 10 years have enabled him to observe first-hand a very frightening development. Many Muslim chaplains are hard at work recruiting Hezbollah, Hamas and Al-Qaeda terrorists within our prisons and, upon the conclusion of their prison terms, inserting them into mainstream society. When it comes to radical Islam, all religions are <u>not</u> equal. It has been hundreds of years since Christianity espoused violence as a way to bring followers to its cause. For Judaism, it has been over 2,000 years. Unfortunately, reformation has not been introduced to Islam. Radical Muslims have no reluctance when it comes to using death, mayhem and violence to promote their ideology.

Chuck Colson confirms that radical Muslims are hard at work in our country's prison system recruiting converts.

> "Alienated, disenfranchised people are prime targets for radical Islamists who preach a religion of violence, of overcoming oppression by Jihad... (T)he radical fundamentalists—some of whom are invading our prisons—mean it literally. Those who take the Koran seriously are taught to hate the Christians and the Jew; lands taken

from Islam must be recaptured. And to
the Islamist, dying in a Jihad is the only
way one can be assured of Allah's for-
giveness and eternal salvation."[lvii]

Chuck Colson states:
"Al Qaeda training manuals specifically
identify *America's prisoners* as candidates for conversion because they may
be 'disenchanted by their country's
policies.' As U.S. citizens, they will
combine a desire for 'payback' with an
ability to blend easily into American
culture."[lviii]

For South Floridians, the story of Jose Padilla and his
conversion to Islam should put every Gold Coast res-
ident on high alert. Padilla was born in 1970 in a
predominantly Hispanic neighborhood in Chicago. At
a young age, Padilla joined a Puerto Rican street gang
known as the "Latin Disciples" and was convicted of
aggravated battery and armed robbery while still a
juvenile. In the fall of 1991, at the age of 21, Jose
Padilla and his family headed to Florida. It wasn't
long until he found himself in a Broward County jail
stemming from a road-rage incident in which he fired
a pistol at another driver.

Upon his release, he got a job at Taco Bell. He was
befriended by the manager of the Taco Bell, a
Muslim-Pakistani immigrant, Mohammad Javed
Qureshi, co-founder of the *Sunrise School of Islamic*

*Studies.* Having been exposed to radical Islam while in prison, Mohammad Qureshi built on the foundation established through the Muslim prison ministry. Padilla was converted to radical Islam at a mosque in Sunrise, Florida in 1994. At the time, the Imam at the mosque was Raed Awad, a fundraiser for the Holy Land Foundation for Relief and Development (HLF) in Florida.[lix] On December 4, 2001, approximately three months after 9/11, HLF was placed in the category of "specially designated global terrorists," pursuant to Executive Order 12947. [lx]

In 1998, Padilla moved to Egypt to learn Arabic and to deepen his understanding of Islam. He then moved to Pakistan, where, before September 11, 2001, Padilla met Zayn al-Abidin Mohammad Husayn Abu Zubaydah. Zubaydah was Osama bin- Laden's chief of military operations for Al-Qaeda. Padilla became Zubaydah's apprentice during 2001-2002 while Zubaydah was organizing the remnants of the Al-Qaeda network scattered by the U.S. attack on Afghanistan. Zubaydah was preparing a plan to detonate a radiological weapon or "dirty bomb" in the United States. (The TV series "24" is more real than you think.) In March 2002, Zubaydah sent Padilla to meet Al-Qaeda leaders and to work with an associate in order to make the bomb. Fortunately, Zubaydah was arrested a few weeks later and was turned over to U.S. authorities. Information obtained from Zubaydah led to Padilla's arrest at O'Hare International Airport after traveling from Pakistan to Zurich, then to Egypt, then back to Zurich, then on to Chicago. He was carrying more than

$10,000 in cash! According to Zubaydah, Padilla had been sent back to the States to find radioactive material that could be used to build a dirty bomb.

Padilla had traveled full circle. Exposed first to radical Islam while in prison he was then recruited in the United States, trained abroad and finally returned to the United States as an Al-Qaeda terrorist, targeting his native country.

The foregoing story, largely untold to the American people by the mainstream press or broadcast media, raises red flags on a number of different levels. First, thank goodness for the Patriot Act which, in its absence, would have made the surveillance and apprehension of both Zubaydah and Padilla improbable. Secondly, it was the prison system which was the incubator and petri dish for the growth of radical Islam within Jose Padilla. Finally, the fact that stories like Jose Padilla are not being told to the American people continues to allow the average American (us) to wallow in our state of denial until it may be too late.

Padilla is an excellent example of what the Islamofascists look for within our United States— minority males, poor, uneducated, alienated, and a history of trouble with authority. Alone and vulnerable in prison, they are easily manipulated and swayed, first into conversion to radical Islam, and ultimately into the violence and death it preaches. There is an ample supply of men fitting this profile throughout America's prison system. There are 5.6 million Americans who are in prison or who have served time in prison. The National Islamic Prison Foundation claims to convert 135,000 prisoners every year. Even if only 10% of such converts subscribe to radical Islam, the number is terrifying.

In light of these alarming statistics, the government (through the Office of Inspector General [OIG]) in April, 2004, prepared a report entitled, "A Review of the Bureau of Prisons' Selection of Muslim Religious Services Providers." OIG identified significant problems related to the selection of Muslim religious service providers: 1) the Bureau of Prisons (BOP) does not examine the doctrinal beliefs of applicants for religious service positions to determine whether those beliefs are consistent or inconsistent with BOP security policies; 2) the BOP and FBI do not adequately exchange information regarding the BOP's endorsing organizations; 3) once contractors and certain volunteers gain access to the Bureau of Prisons facilities, ample opportunity exists for them to deliver extremist messages without supervision from BOP staff; 4) BOP inmates frequently lead Islamic religious services with only minimal supervision from BOP staff members, enhancing the likelihood that seditious, treasonous or inappropriate content can be delivered to the inmates.[lxi]

When vetting potential Muslim chaplains, the BOP does not ask them whether they have received funds from foreign governments or whether they have spent time in a country that does not have diplomatic relations or treaties with the United States. In Ohio, an Ohio State prisons report concluded that conversion to

Islam had led some inmates to become members of terrorist groups, including Hezbollah.[lxii]

At a time when we should be watching the prison system with greater scrutiny, the Islamofascists' unwitting collaborators, the A.C.L.U., is doing all it can to oppose the scrutiny.[lxiii] The reader can conduct further research in accordance with the footnotes cited here, but here is something you are not likely to see reported in the mainstream media: a warning from the OIG's report after a review of the "Federal Bureau of Prisons' Selection of Muslim Religious Services Providers,"

> The presence of extremist chaplains, contractors, or volunteers in the BOP's correctional facilities can pose a threat to institutional security and could implicate national security if inmates are encouraged to commit terrorist acts against the United States. For this reason, it is imperative that the BOP has in place sound screening and supervision practices that will identify persons that seek to disrupt the order of its institutions or to inflict harm on the United States through terrorism.[lxiv]

## 5. AMERICAN NAIVETÉ

Fortunately, as more and more information is published by the private sector concerning the Islamic threat faced by all, the ignorance and naïveté of the

American citizenry is diminishing. However, this book is written because I am convinced that the vast majority of Americans are still largely uninformed about the threat we face. There are three informational outlets that can be doing more to forewarn Americans: 1) other than Fox News and Glenn Beck on CNN, the silence of the mainstream media is deafening; 2) The political correctness and "tolerance" of our higher educational institutions; 3) The unwillingness of the Bush administration to identify or even acknowledge to the American people that this Islamofascist ideology not only exists, but is a clear and present danger to all of us. Most Americans remain in the dark. WAKE UP, AMERICA!

It does appear that some of our leaders are beginning to sit up and take notice. In January 2007, both the U.S. House of Representatives and Senate have organized caucuses on anti-terrorism. Congresswoman Sue Myrick from North Carolina has been and is a strong voice crying in the wilderness about the threat we face. In interviewing a number of people both inside and outside of government, (who have asked to remain anonymous) it is estimated that 50% to 80% of all mosques in the United States are fronts for terrorist cells in the United States. Such mosques are not teaching religion; but rather an ideology of hate, masquerading as a religion. Islam has been hijacked by radicals. The radicals are in charge of the educational and news media infrastructure in the Middle East. The radicals are in charge of the majority of the mosques in the United States. Mosques in Falls

Church, Virginia, Los Angeles, California, Brooklyn, New York, Boca Raton, Florida, and other places are hotbeds for sedition in the name of Islam.

Fortunately, not all elements of the government are unable or unwilling to confront terrorism within the United States. In June of 2006, the Department of Justice published its White Paper on Terrorism, reporting that since 9/11 there have been over 450 prosecutions for terrorism, over 200 of which have resulted in convictions. Do not be mislead into believing that the capture of bin Laden will end the terrorist threat. Al-Qaeda is only one arm of the Muslim terrorist ideology that is spreading with each passing day.

## ENDING AMERICAN NAIVETÉ

First and foremost, every American needs to be informed. Knowledge is power; awareness is the first step of self-defense. No treatment can begin for a disease until it is recognized and diagnosed. Similarly, no battle can be fought until the enemy is clearly understood. This is not a war on terror. Islam is a religion; Islamofascism is an ideology. Al-Qaeda, Hezbollah, and Hamas all subscribe to the same ideology. We must stop allowing our political leaders and journalists to fail to identify, and inaccurately describe, the war that America faces. The main reason Americans continue to be naïve and uninformed about the Islamofascist threat is because our politicians and journalists through the demands of "political correctness" are constrained from accurately describing the war embroiling America. As

Harvey Kushner eloquently stated, "Political correctness has made us so afraid of being branded racist that we force ourselves to be colorblind, identity-blind and gender-blind until we end up, quite simply, totally blind."[lxv] This is a fight to the death. For the first time in about 200 years, America must come to grips with the fact that it is and will be fighting a war on its own soil, on its own turf. The war is here; the war is now. Will we prevail?

# CHAPTER 6
# TOLERANCE IS CULTURAL SUICIDE WHEN IT'S A ONE-WAY STREET

*Dancing with the devil of destruction*

TOLERANCE—Motherhood, apple pie, the American tradition of assimilation of immigrants. Who, other than unrepentant racists, could suggest that tolerance is not a good thing?

But, as this concept has evolved and morphed over the last twenty years, it is time to re-examine whether "tolerance" has become a Trojan Horse; something allowed into our culture without objection, but something that will eventually be used to destroy us. Harsh, you say?

To examine "tolerance" and the danger that this concept now poses to our way of life, one must first look back, then one must look to where we are today, and finally, one must look ahead to see where the trends of tolerance are taking us in the not- too-distant future.

## THE WAY WE WERE

It was less than a generation ago when time off from school classes for public school students during the latter part of December, was called "Christmas Vacation." Somewhere along the line it became "Winter Break," so as to be tolerant of those that did not celebrate Christmas. Now, even Christian Schools denote the two weeks off in late December and early January as "Winter Break."

There was a time when Christmas carols were routinely sung in our public schools in December. After all, it was the Christmas season. Now public schools no longer allow the children to sing Christmas songs that have overtly religious tones and in many schools today, Christmas songs are banned altogether, even "Rudolph the Red-Nosed Reindeer." "Silent Night" has truly become silent. Culturally, the only reason the December vacation existed was to coincide with the celebration of the birth of Christ. Today, "tolerance" can't or won't acknowledge the cultural roots of the holiday. Very recently, some schools in the Northeast have been labeling the two weeks of vacation in December the "Winter Solstice," reverting to the pagan holiday that existed around December 21st, two thousand years ago.

Remember when your City Hall was actually allowed to have "Christmas" decorations? But demands were made to remove from the public square any displays that might disclose the religious origin of the holiday season in December.

It was a generation ago, or less, when the ten days of vacation for students in March or April of every year was denoted "Easter Vacation." With the help of Hollywood, Annette Funicello and Fort Lauderdale Beach, the tolerant crowd won a permanent victory in renaming Easter Vacation, "Spring Break."

Anyone (reading this book) who is over 50 years old can remember reciting the "Our Father" in school every day. Many of you remember the Ten Commandments that adorned your school hallway. The prayer is silenced and the Ten Commandments are erased. And now at graduation time, in our zeal to be tolerant of all citizens, no prayer can be uttered in thanks for the accomplishments of the graduating students. So now a student in an Arizona high school has composed his own:

### The New School Prayer

Now I sit me down in school
Where praying is against the rule
For this great nation under God
Finds mention of Him very odd.
If Scripture now the class recites,
It violates the Bill of Rights.
And anytime my head I bow
Becomes a Federal matter now.
Our hair can be purple, orange or green,
That's no offense; it's a freedom scene.

The law is specific, the law is precise:
Prayers spoken aloud are a serious vice.
For praying in a public hall
Might offend someone with no faith at all.
In silence alone we must meditate,
God's name is prohibited by the state.
We're allowed to cuss and dress like freaks,
And pierce our noses, tongues and cheeks.
They've outlawed guns, but FIRST the Bible.
To quote the Good Book makes me liable.
We can elect a pregnant Senior Queen,
And the 'unwed daddy,' our Senior King.
It's "inappropriate" to teach right from wrong,
We're taught that such "judgments" do not belong.
We can get our condoms and birth controls,
Study witchcraft, vampires and totem poles.
But the Ten Commandments are not allowed,
No word of God much reach this crowd.
It's scary here, I must confess,
When chaos reigns the school's a mess.
So, Lord, this silent plea I make:
Should I be shot; My soul please take!
Amen.[lxvi]

Our Founding Fathers' documents establishing the birth of this country are replete with thanks to a higher power for His blessings and replete with requests to His power for guidance and deliverance for a nation they conceived in liberty. In 2006, a federal judge in Kentucky actually entered an injunction forbidding high school students from praying at their

graduation! The fact that the graduating seniors bla-
tantly disobeyed the court mandate and recited the
Lord's Prayer in unison at the graduation ceremony
should be great comfort to those who believe that we,
as a nation, are not yet in the end stages of cultural
suicide. Perhaps the rise of this next generation,
dubbed the "new millennials" will restore common
sense to our body politic.

## THE WAY WE ARE

How many people have now succumbed to wishing
everyone "Happy Holidays," so as to be tolerant of
those that do not celebrate Christmas? When
Americans forego "Merry Christmas" as though that
term were offensive, tolerance becomes cultural suicide in light of the fact that 85% of Americans still
identify themselves as Christians. Indeed, cultural
suicide is well on its way in America when "Merry
Christmas" becomes politically incorrect.

Unfortunately, this quest for a utopian society
based on the false notion of tolerance has percolated
up and out of the schools and into our mainstream
culture. Even worse, it has mutated into an <u>intoler-
ance</u> of traditional sacredness. So-called art, funded
with your tax dollars, pays for a picture of a crucifix
in a jar of urine, entitled "Piss Christ," and is displayed to the public in the Brooklyn Museum of Art.
More recently, a parody of the President was painted
on a mural showing him being sodomized by Osama
bin Laden over a barrel of oil. You do not have to be
a supporter of the President to be viscerally offended

by your tax money supporting that kind of art in a time of war.

But reverse intolerance is manifested in much less offensive ways when, for example, Condoleezza Rice, the Secretary of State of the United States is invited to be the commencement speaker at Boston College and is vehemently opposed by its faculty and students; but Ward Churchill, a radical American hater, and a professor from the University of Colorado is welcomed at the same university. Tolerance is cultural suicide when it's a one-way street.

## TOLERANCE CHANGES THE WAY NEWS IS REPORTED

"Tolerance" so as not to offend Muslims affects the way Islamic violence is reported. It is absurd and dangerous because the average American is lulled into a false sense of security, hence the reason for writing this book. Remember the terrorists who seized a theater in Moscow in 2002 resulting in the tragic deaths of many Russian innocents? They were Islamic terrorists. However, the *New York Times* referred to them as "separatists" and "guerillas."

Remember the kid from California, John Walker Lindh, who fought for the Taliban and was caught by U.S. troops? Well it turns out that he had actually changed his name in high school to Suleyman Al-Lindh. When he was captured by American forces he was known by the name of Abdul Hameed. Although it had been <u>years</u> since he was John Walker, that was the only name the "tolerant" press used for him.

Remember the shoe bomber on the plane? The

press called him "Richard Reed." However, the name he responded to when he tried to bomb the plane was Abdul Rahim. The French police identified him as Tariq Raga, yet the tolerant press only referred to him as Richard Reed.

Remember the Washington D.C. snipers? The elder sniper had converted to Islam 17 years prior, had changed his name to John Mohammad, and belonged to Louis Farrakhan's Nation of Islam. CNN, however, initially reported his name as John Allan Williams and a "Gulf War Veteran."

More recently, when the 17 terrorists were arrested in Canada, the *New York Times* described them as "Southern Asians" rather than that they all belonged to the Nation of Islam, the real truth.

As recently as October 22, 2006, in a report on anger and resentment still festering in French areas scarred by the riots of 2005, both the *New York Times* and the *Baltimore Sun* reported on an ambush of police in a Paris suburb. The *New York Times* reported the perpetrators as "unemployed, undereducated youths, mostly the offspring of Arab and African immigrants." The *Baltimore Sun* reported the truth: the rioting was by "Muslim immigrants from North Africa…" The *New York Times* refuses to identify the perpetrators or speak the truth.

The tolerant crowd should heed well this advice: When in doubt about the proper orientation of your moral compass, point it away from the people that want to behead you. Tolerance, it seems, has an evil twin – an inability to discern what cannot be tolerated. (Alas, the sheep refuse or don't want to recognize the presence of wolves.)

So if this trend continues, where are we headed?

## THE JUDGE AND THE CROSS

Judge Stableman could not believe the headline in the *New England Constitution*, the newspaper of choice for his community: *"Judge to be indicted for hate crime."*

*How had it come to this?* he thought to himself. His law school record had been stellar. He qualified for *The Law Review*, and upon graduation took a position as a highly paid associate at one of the more high- profile law firms in the state. After toiling for six years as an associate, he was made a fast-track partner. Shortly after, however, he eschewed the opportunity for extraordinary wealth, and answered a higher calling to put on the black robe in order to make a difference in the community which he loved.

He began his judicial career as a gubernatorial appointee to the bench. He was able to use the connections from his law firm to wrangle an appointment over other more experienced, perhaps more qualified lawyer applicants. He began his judicial career with the County Court, handling misdemeanors, traffic offenses and small claims suits. He soon distinguished himself by his courtroom demeanor, quick wit and the ability to zero- in on issues quickly.

After a few years, he was promoted to a higher trial court which dealt only with felony crimes and civil cases where more than $75,000 was at stake. He attended church regularly with his wife and two children. After eight years on the trial bench, everyone assumed it was only a matter of time before his elevation to an appellate court became a reality. And then, Christmas of 2011 came along. Of course, by 2011 what had traditionally been called the "Christmas" season was now referred to as the "Winter Solstice" holiday.

By 2011, Judge Stableman's wife, Pamela wanted her two children to have a Winter Solstice season that was all about Christmas. She was raising the children as Christians but dutifully sent James and Heather to public school so that they would have the chance to experience other students with diverse cultures, backgrounds and religious beliefs. Now that they were getting older, however, she was concerned that the children were completely forgetting the "reason for the season." Public schools had long since jettisoned the singing of "Christmas" songs, since it was determined that even such innocuous songs as "Rudolph the Red- Nosed Reindeer" reminded children of the Christmas holiday, which could be deemed offensive to atheists or other non-Christian religions.

So this year, Pamela decided to decorate the house differently. She kept the plastic Santa and the plastic Frosty the Snowman in the attic. She made a trip in early December to the local Christian supply center in order to purchase more meaningful holiday decorations. The trip was an ordeal. She had to drive 45 minutes each way and it took a long time and a lot of money to choose and purchase just the right decorations. Three years before, when the local Wal-Mart, Target and JCPenney stores stopped carrying traditional Christmas decorations, she was in agreement with the other members of the PTA who thought it was a good idea. Muslims had begun to boycott the stores for carrying such items, but Pamela Stableman understood how a Muslim walking into a store filled with Christmas displays could be hurt and offended.

Thirty minutes into her trip to the Christian supply center, though, Pamela began to resent Wal-Mart and the Muslims, whom she now blamed for causing her to make this 90-minute trip during a time of the year that was busy with <u>so</u> much to do. As she was driving, she thought about the Solstice celebration she had promised to attend and the Solstice cookies she had promised to bake for the party. The traffic was worse than she had anticipated and now it looked like she would not get the cookies baked. Mrs. Stableman fretted over arriving at the party empty- handed. She concluded the trip was worth it, however, because both Heather and James needed to see how front lawns used to be decorated when she was a little girl.

She hadn't really discussed the whole project with her husband, but she was confident he would agree it was a good idea, even though he was a judge. She knew her husband was very sensitive to diverse peoples and cultures. He had made a point many times of not going forward with court hearings or trials when dealing with defendants or litigants whose first language was not English. He had even delayed a trial for months one time so that the Defendant could obtain (at state expense) an interpreter for an Afghan Muslim from the northeast region of that country who spoke a unique dialect of Farsi.

When she arrived at the "Christmas" store, the inventory and displays took her breath away. Happy memories of her childhood came flooding back to her. In her mind's eye she saw her mom and grandma laughing like schoolgirls as they shopped for an extra knick-knack so the house would be just so. "Don't leave the 'Christ' out of Christmas," her mother would say. She fought back tears, then became embarrassed when the sales clerk approached. Noticing that her teary eyes caught the clerk's attention, Pamela apologized.

"I'm sorry. It's just that ..."

"Oh, don't even think about that," said the nice clerk, "almost everyone that comes in here gets all sentimental, remembering how it used to be."

Driving into her neighborhood, Pamela was most pleased with herself. She had obtained a stable containing a solar light sensor that would illuminate automatically after dark. The scene included some barnyard animals, Mary, Joseph and the manger containing Jesus. She found a star that was attached to a titanium pole that, once assembled, would hover thirty feet over the manger scene and would be visible throughout the neighborhood. At the last minute, Pamela decided to buy something else that, although it was not very common when she was a child, she thought in this day and age might be appropriate. Mrs.

Stableman purchased an 8' x 6' white cross that would also be illuminated at night. Since they were going to have "Christmas" decorations this year, she thought they might as well go "all the way." As Pamela pulled into the driveway that afternoon, she could hardly contain her exuberance. Her excitement was contagious as both Heather and James become excited over the prospect of having a unique Solstice display in their front yard. Not one house in the area would be decorated like this. They were in the process of assembling the scene when Judge Stableman came home.

"What do we have here?" he asked, noticing that that the faded Santa Claus and carrot-nosed Frosty the Snowman were not on display.

"Well this year, honey, I decided we would have real 'Christmas' decorations. The kids are getting older and other than once a year in church, they have really never experienced "Christmas." So I got the stable, the manger and Mary and Joseph, and once this cross is assembled, it's going to be eight feet high! And the star that the three wise men followed— well, people are going to be able to see that for blocks!"

"Well, that sounds pretty cool," responded Judge Stableman.

The kids rolled their eyeballs. "Why does Dad use such old-fashioned expressions? Nobody says 'cool' anymore," they thought to themselves.

Judge Stableman went inside with his briefcase full of work while Pamela and the children finished the display. When it was done, it was a sight to behold.

None of the neighbors could remember when someone had a manger scene in their front yard for the
Winter Solstice season, and the star was actually
visible for miles. The light from the cross illuminated
the entire front yard. It wasn't long before word
spread, and night after night cars would drive by just
to get a glimpse of the display. Despite the cold
weather, some folks actually parked and got out of
their cars to gaze at the sight.

On some nights when Pamela wasn't that busy,
she would come out to chat with a few of what her
kids called "the gawkers." Pamela noticed that tears
welled up in many eyes as folks marveled at the sight.
Judge Stableman seemed oblivious to the new-found
commotion on 1953 Elm Street, New Canaan,
Connecticut.

Then one night, two days before Christmas but
two days after the Winter Solstice (the Solstice
traditionally being celebrated on December 21st, and
the unofficial holiday of "Christmas" being celebrated on December 25th), inside the Stableman house
the phone rang. Pamela and the children were outside
talking to the "gawkers" passing by, so Judge
Stableman answered the phone.

"Hello?"

"This is Joe Mumford." Joe Mumford was a
political insider who had helped Judge Stableman get
his appointment as a County Court Judge from the
governor's office and later an appointment to the
Circuit Court.

"Oh, hi Joe, how are you?"

"I'm okay but you're not. Your Solstice display is causing quite a commotion."

"Why is that, Joe?"

"Crap, Judge, don't you know that you have Muslims that live right next door?"

"Yea, so?"

"What do you mean, 'yea, so'? Your star and cross are driving them nuts. They don't celebrate Christmas, and your display is like shoving it right down their throats. You are totally in their face."

"Aw, Joe, you're overreacting. I know Mr. Mamoud. We've always gotten along great. Whenever the hedge between our houses gets too high, he pays for the hedge-trimmer guy one year and I pay for him the next. Just because he doesn't celebrate Christmas, what's the big deal?"

"Judge, I think you've been out of politics too long. They filed a complaint with the American Civil Liberties Union, and the ACLU has asked for a criminal investigation."

"A criminal investigation? What are you talking about?"

"What I'm talking about, Judge, is a Hate Crime. You, more than anybody else ought to know what a Hate Crime is. You can't do anything that might offend somebody who doesn't have the same beliefs as you. Listen Judge, I know you're on the civil side of the courthouse right now but you used to be on the criminal side. You need to be aware."

"Yea, I know, Joe, but when I presided on the criminal side the Hate Crime legislation hadn't been passed yet."

"Well, Judge, you need to pay attention because one, you have Muslims that live next door; two, you have a display on your front yard that is overtly Christian; and three, you should know that any overtly Christian display on your front yard is going to offend your non-Christian next door neighbor. That's a Hate Crime, Judge."

"Well, Joe, I appreciate your concern, but I think you're overreacting. Don't forget, five years ago I received the 'Jurist of the Year' award from the Muslim-American Relations Foundation when I insisted that there be Arabic translators in the courthouse for all criminal proceedings. Besides, Mamoud is a good guy, and I don't see any problem. Good-bye, Joe. And by the way, Merry Christmas."

"Geez, Judge, take it easy with that stuff, will you? Good-bye."

The Judge walked outside to talk to Pamela. As he walked up to the manger scene, a family who had just parked their car got out. It was obviously a mother and father and their three kids. But the Judge didn't recognize them. He was approached by the father.

"Hey, you're Judge Stableman, aren't you? Well I just want you to know, Judge, that this is the greatest Christmas display I've seen in a long time. My kids go to school down at Apple Blossom Elementary, and when I heard about your display I had to bring them by. Nobody has displays like this anymore, Judge, and I just want you to know... you're my hero."

Judge Stableman mumbled a "thank you," but was completely taken aback by the father's response. His initial thought was, "What is this guy talking about? I'm no hero."

The man corralled his family back into the car, rolled down his window and as he drove away said, "Keep it up, Judge, you're the best." Judge Stableman's thoughts did not dwell on the nice man.

"Pam, I just received a phone call from Joe. He's concerned about our display."    "Honey," his wife responded, "We've received more compliments about this display than you can possibly imagine! Heather and James are all the rage at their school and they've been asked to give talks in their civics class about free speech...whatever that's about."

"But Pam, Joe seems concerned that we might be offending the Mamouds with this display."

"For having a manger scene in our front yard?" Pamela asked. "Oh, come on, sweetie, you know Joe, he always overreacts. Political consultants are too cautious."

Judge Stableman walked away. His wife's common sense was convincing.

The whole thing had died down by the time February, 2012 came around. Then the phone call came on the Friday before Presidents' weekend. It was Joe.

"Judge, you didn't listen to me. I told you, but you didn't listen to me!"

"What, Joe, what?"

"You're going to be indicted Judge, and the Judicial Qualifications Commission is going to look into your fitness to continue to be a judge."

"What are you talking about?"

"Judge, the holiday display, remember? You have the whole Muslim community in New Canaan outraged. Now they even want to have the name of the town changed, since "Canaan" is a biblical name. I don't know if I can help you on this one. The political damage is too great. I think in order to protect the governor, you're going to have to resign…"

The newspaper arrived the next morning….

## PART 3
## IT'S MORE REAL THAN YOU THINK

The nightmare scenario that you've just read is more real than you might think. I attended law school at the University of Miami. I received an excellent education and my law degree has served me well. Unfortunately, the higher educational climate in Miami has changed in the 30 years since I lived there and attended school. Miami was, and to a large extent still is, populated by people with a great love of freedom and appreciation for the United States, as there are thousands of residents of Cuban descent who fled their Cuban homeland to seek a better way of life for themselves and their families.

Recently, however, at Florida International University, the Genocide Awareness Project (GAP) placed posters depicting forms of genocide throughout history next to pictures of unborn babies. The FIU school newspaper in response said, "Whoever these people are, they should be shot." So much for tolerance and the free exchange of ideas at our institutions of "higher" learning.[lxvii] Abraham Lincoln once said, "The philosophy of the schoolroom in one generation becomes the philosophy of the government in the next."[lxviii]

Michelle Shocks of Seattle was riding home on a bus one day when another passenger boarded, saying "Praise the Lord!" He was happy to be out of the pouring rain. The two started to privately discuss religion across the aisle. The bus driver could overhear them, however, and ordered them to stop their discussion because it might "offend" other passengers. Michelle moved to a seat next to the recently boarded passenger and they continued their discussion in hushed tones. The driver pulled to the side of the road and demanded that both passengers leave the bus. Michelle, who was 25 years old and 5 months pregnant, was forced to walk the last mile to her home (in the rain).[lxix]

The American Bar Association proposed a change to its ethics rules in August of 2004 suggesting that judicial candidates and judges be forced to quit groups like the Boy Scouts or be removed from the bench. The Boy Scouts, you ask? Yes, because the Scouts refuse to allow homosexual scoutmasters.[lxx]

The law is changing before our eyes. Slowly, insidiously, our freedoms are being taken away. A radical assault on American values has taken place over the last 40 years. It has gone largely unreported in the mainstream media.

Below is a brief survey of recent Court decisions that have changed our country and our traditional American values. After reading what follows, ask yourself if the fictional story you just read is not far off.

Verbal prayer in our public schools has been declared unconstitutional, even if that prayer is both voluntary and denominationally neutral. See *Engle v. Vitale,* 370 U.S. 421, (1962); *Abington v. Schempp,* 374 U.S. 203, (1963).

In *Reed v. Van Hoven,* 237 F. Supp. 48, (W. D. Mich., 1965), it was decided that if a student prays over his lunch it is unconstitutional for him to pray out loud.

When a student in a public school addresses an assembly of his peers he effectively becomes a government representative and it is therefore unconstitutional for that student to engage in prayer. See *Harris v. Joint School District,* 41 F.3rd 447, (9th Cir., 1994).

In 1999, in the case of *Rubin v. City of Burbank,* 101 Cal. App. 4th 1194, (2002) the court decided that a City Council meeting can offer prayer, so long as the council does not offer the name of Jesus.

In *Gierke v. Blotzer,* CV-88-0-883, USDC Neb., 1989, a student in Omaha, Nebraska was prohibited from reading his bible silently during study hall and was even enjoined from opening his bible at school.

The case of *Roberts v. Madigan,* 921 F. 2nd 1047, (10th Cir., 1990) declared it to be unconstitutional for a classroom library to contain books that deal with Christianity or for a teacher to be seen with a personal copy of his or her bible at school.

With regard to crosses, it has been declared unconstitutional for a public cemetery to have a planter in the shape of a cross, for if someone were to view that cross, such viewing could cause emotional distress and injury. *Warsaw v. Tehachapi,* CV-F-90-404 USDC, E. D. Cal, 1990.

In June, 2004, the Los Angeles County Supervisors voted 3-2 to remove a tiny cross from the official County Seal rather than face a potential lawsuit from the ACLU. The cross had been on the County Seal for 47 years!

"The philosophy of the schoolroom in one generation becomes the philosophy of the government in the next."

On September 22, 2004, under California Law SB1234, individuals can now claim that someone expressing their deeply-held religious beliefs present an "intimidating threat."[lxxi]

Canada recently passed a hate crimes law which has been dubbed the "Bible as hate literature bill." It makes public criticism of homosexuality a crime.[lxxii]

Ask yourself this question: Is the indictment of Judge Stableman all that unrealistic?

TOLERANCE IS CULTURAL SUICIDE WHEN IT IS A ONE-WAY STREET.

# CHAPTER 7
# WILL JUDEO-CHRISTIANITY SURVIVE?

*"America — the last, best hope of man on Earth."*
— *Ronald Reagan*

It seems everywhere Islam goes, violence follows. Violence continues to rage in Afghanistan as the Taliban refuse to go quietly. In December, 2006, the Taliban were murdering teachers, mostly young women, as collaborators in the new government, the participants of which are branded as infidels. In Iran, where there is a particularly virulent form of Islamic fascism, the ruling Islamic fascists are on a collision course with Israel and the United States over nuclear weapons (Umm, uranium enrichment). Somalia's top Islamic leader, on July 21, 2006, called for a holy war against Ethiopia to drive out troops the largely

Christian nation (Ethiopia) sent to protect the internationally-backed Somali government. In Lebanon, Hezbollah and Hamas fight each other, Israelis, Americans, and the West. In Iraq, both Shiite and Sunni mosques are struck with bombs and mortars. And when the radicals (no "insurgents") are not killing each other, they are targeting Americans or any "infidel" that wants to bring democracy to that country. In Sri Lanka, government troops clash with Tamil tiger "rebels." The rebels are Islamists. In Pakistan, a suicide bomber blows himself up outside the home of a prominent Shiite Muslim cleric triggering a riot in Karachi. In India, bombers attacked Bombay's rail system. More Islamic violence is on the way. In Nigeria, Islamic forces kill Christians on sight. In the Sudan, in the Darfur region, ethnic cleansing is still ongoing. Chechnya "rebels" in Russia kill women and children. The "rebels" are Islamic fascists, despite the fact that the news media refuses to identify them as such. Islamic fascists blow up trains in Spain, riot in France, blow up buses and trains in London and are caught in Canada before having the opportunity to do the same. Yet the news media asks, "Why Canada? They have never supported the United States in its war in Afghanistan or Iraq and Canada has a very open-door immigration policy towards Muslims." Those who ask that question don't get it.

Former Senator Rick Santorum gets it. In a speech delivered on July 20, 2006, he stated, "The biggest issue facing our children's future is a war. Not as so many describe it, the War on Terror. Not the war in Iraq or Afghanistan. But the world war, which at its heart, is just like the previous three global struggles."[lxxiii] The Senator is referring to the war with Islamofascism.

In World War II we fought German Nazis and Japanese imperialists. Today, we fight Islamic fascists. Consider also the citizens of Australia, Indonesia, Thailand, Egypt and Argentina. Those countries, too, have suffered firsthand and mourned innocent victims as a result of terrorism at the hands of Islamofascists.

Ronald Reagan branded Communism as an "Evil Empire." All enlightened people understood that Nazism was an evil, racist regime. We must understand with moral clarity this war against Islamofascism. Our failure to appreciate the danger entails the ultimate price: that the United States, or even Judeo-Christianity, will not survive.

## THE ISLAMIC MESSIAH

Islam's aggression into the West began during the period of what Westerners were taught were the "Dark Ages." The aggression began in the 7$^{th}$ Century and ended on September 11, 1683, when the siege of Vienna by the Muslims finally ceased. Centuries passed. On September 11, 2001, the siege began anew—a different type of siege, but a siege no less. Jihad can be loosely translated as "my inner struggle," or "my struggle." The leader of Iran has stated that he will wipe Israel and the United States "off the face of the earth." Ahmadinejad believes world conflict is necessary in order to bring about the Islamic end times and to pave the way for the Sh'ia Muslim Messiah, the 12th Imam.

In a November 16, 2005 speech in Tehran to senior clerics who had come from all over Iran to hear him, Ahmadinejad, the President of Iran, stated that the main mission of his government was to "pave the way for the glorious reappearance of Imam Mahdi (may God hasten his reappearance)."[lxxiv] The mystical 12th Imam of Sh'ia Islam is venerated by many in Iran. He disappeared as a child in 941 C.E. and Sh'ia Muslims have been awaiting his reappearance ever since. They believe that when he returns he will reign on earth for seven years, bringing about the last judgment and the end of the world as we know it.

In September 2006, Ahmadinejad finished his U.N. speech with a prayer for the imminent coming of the 12th Imam, whom he called "a perfect human being who is heir to all prophets and pious men." The Ahmadinejad cabinet has allocated $17 million to renovate the Jamkarin mosque, where devotees of the 12th Imam have come to pray for centuries. Ahmadinejad has told regime officials that the hidden Imam will reappear in <u>two years</u>. Devotees of the 12th Imam believe that only increased violence, conflict and oppression will bring about the Mahdi's return. Since assuming power in Iran, Ahmadinejad has placed 12th Imam devotees in his cabinet and throughout the bureaucracy. Concurrently, Ahmadinejad is moving aggressively to stop the proliferation of Christian house churches throughout the country. He has stated, "I will stop Christianity in this country." A religious zealot with nuclear weapons, vowing to destroy Israel and the United States, is a dangerous combination. Will Judeo-Christianity survive?

## THE ISLAMIC STATES OF AMERICA [lxxv]– CIRCA 2039

The U.N. General Assembly rose in unison to applaud the announcement by the Ambassador to the U.N. from the Islamic States of America (I.S.A.) that the "Bible Belt Rebellion," as the uprising had been dubbed, was finally subdued after three years of violence. The I.S.A.'s ambassador to the U.N. gave a brief history of the conflict when he made his announcement.

"In 2036, we expected more tolerance from the radical Christian groups that formerly controlled parts of Louisiana, Mississippi, Alabama, Georgia, North Florida, the Carolinas, Tennessee, Arkansas and West Virginia. But when those states refused to accept the national Muslim curriculum and the national school dress code, (enacted so that no child would be left in ignorance) we had no choice but to send in federal Marshals."

To many, the deployment of federal Marshals to quell the violence in 2036 recalled the days of the civil rights movement of the 1960's. This time, 75 years later, federal Marshals were brought in to restore order and keep the peace so as to enforce the new national dress code for all public schools, requiring, for example, that all girls cover their faces. When the federal Marshals showed up to keep the peace and enforce the new enlightened policy, a clearly organized rebellion attacked and killed the Marshals throughout the region.

"The intolerant Christians hid for years in the Appalachian Mountains." The Ambassador continued his report to the General Assembly of the United Nations: "Yesterday, we captured and killed the leader of the rebellion, Thomas Cromwell. His militia surrendered soon after."

The applause that swept the General Assembly, now located in Copenhagen, the capital of the Eurabia Union, was deafening.

The Islamic States of America Ambassador continued, "In accordance with international law, we will seek the death penalty for all involved. We would like the beheadings of those responsible to serve as an example to all intolerant Christians throughout the region that no disobedience to our duly-elected Caliphate-President will be sanctioned."

Many in the audience remembered the United States of America before it became the Islamic States of America. About 20 years before, the world was fed up with America's intolerant, warlike foreign policy. The Zionist-Christian warlords in America believed they were invincible. But one day in 2013, everything changed for the Zionist-Imperialist country. The electorate in 2012 had finally voted the aggressors out of office. The New Democrat Peace Party assumed power and immediately announced plans to withdraw all troops in any locations which were deemed hostile to the Muslim community. It was commonly believed that Muslim violence against America was simply the result of American military presence in Muslim countries. The prevailing thought, especially in the State Department, was that only after the withdrawal of American troops could relations with Muslim countries begin to normalize. Then dialogue for peaceful coexistence could begin. Iranian President-for-Life, Mahmoud Ahmadinejad, praised the new administration for its clear vision and sound judgment. Most rejoiced as the new administration brought peace with honor to the United States. On September 30, 2013, the last C5A Galaxy carrying the last company of combat troops left a small oil-rich country in the Middle East.

By December 6, 2013, it had almost been a year since the New Democrat Peace Party had been in control. Americans had become supremely confident in their exercise of good judgment in electing new leaders espousing peace. Most Americans, in and out of government had long since forgotten the report by the *New York Times* on March 31, 2007. The Energy Department Inspector General reported that the office in charge of protecting American technical secrets about nuclear weapons from foreign spies was missing 20 desktop computers. In fact, it was the 13th time in four years that an audit found the department, whose national laboratories and factories did most of the work in designing and building nuclear warheads, had lost control of the computers used in working on the bombs. Nobody seemed overly concerned as peace demonstrations overshadowed any concerns for national security.

It took the thieves about six years to perfect the designs taken from the stolen information and to manufacture the bombs. On the evening of December 6, 2013, a junior analyst in the National Security Agency (NSA) was going over routine satellite images of ship movements in the Atlantic and Pacific within 500 miles of the American coast.[lxxvi] The analyst thought he saw something unusual in the photos and called his supervisor over to talk. "Look," he said gesturing at the photos posted on several computer screens. "See these boats? They look like fishing trawlers or private yachts. They've been moving in along shipping lanes for several days, across the South Pacific toward the West Coast, and up from the South Atlantic toward the East Coast. They are all small and slow, but if you look at the times and courses, it appears that they are all going to approach our coastlines at about the same time and will all be about the same distance off the coast at the same time." The Supervisor said, "They're fishing boats. Don't worry about it."

At 2:00 p.m. on December 7, 2013, the first of six cruise missiles to hit the Washington, D.C. area exploded about 500 feet above the White House. 1600 Pennsylvania Avenue was vaporized, along with the President and her entire cabinet. Five other missiles reached their destinations shortly thereafter. One over the Pentagon; one over the C.I.A. in Langley, Virginia; one over the U.S. Capitol; one over F.B.I. headquarters and one over the Supreme Court. In just a matter of minutes, 250,000 people were dead or dying in the Washington, D.C. area and the United States government was decapitated. At about the same time, missiles exploded over the New York Stock Exchange in New York City, the financial district of Boston, the Norfolk, Virginia Naval Base and Baltimore Harbor.

On the West Coast, the same type of short-range nuclear cruise missiles exploded over Los Angeles, San Francisco, the Silicon Valley of Santa Clara County, and Sacramento, California. The Northwest coastal cities were not overlooked. Portland, Oregon and Seattle, Washington were also destroyed.

The missiles were less than 20 feet long and only 18 inches in diameter, powered by small fuel-efficient high octane turbo fans painted in light blue and light gray, flying at a low altitude to avoid detection. They were state-of-the-art designs ten years before. In January, 2007 the Administrator of the National Nuclear Security Agency, the Energy Department in charge of the bombs, had been fired because of the theft scandals, but now seven years later, it became apparent the action was too little and too late.

The attacks came from old fishing trawlers using launch tubes that could be dismantled and stored in the holds under ice and fish. As soon as each boat had launched its pair of missiles, the crew abandoned each trawler, quickly moving into rubber inflatable boats. Just before the last man was over the side, the timer was started on the explosive devices rigged on each trawler. Five miles away and 15 minutes later, each crew member was climbing up the nets on the side of a small freighter of Liberian registry, where each man was issued new identification as the ship's crew. The rubber inflatables were shot and sunk at the same time the charges placed in the bilges of each of the fishing trawlers exploded, sending any evidence of the attacks to the bottom of the ocean. With no obvious enemy to blame, fingers pointed in every direction.

By Christmas, the American economy was destroyed. Inflation soared as the government printed money to meet its responsibilities without sufficient economic output to back the issuance of the currency. Unemployment soared as major centers of employment had been incinerated by the nuclear blasts. Businesses throughout the United States closed. Tax revenues evaporated, so state governments had no funds to pay unemployment benefits or teachers' salaries. For the first time in U.S. history, both state and federal governments defaulted on their bond obligations. U.S. creditor nations called their loans. With the New York Stock Exchange gone and all of its records destroyed with it, stock trading ended and stock values plummeted. Retirement assets and pension funds disappeared virtually overnight. The population was in complete chaos. The real estate market crashed, major banks filed for bankruptcy and riots broke out throughout the country as panic set in. With the collapse of the American economy, which was the largest on earth, responsible for producing one-third of global economic output, the rest of the global economy also fell into chaos. Oil shipments stopped, food shipments stopped, and millions of people began to starve throughout the world.

With the President dead, the Vice-President, who had been vacationing in Colorado, assumed control of what was left of the American government. Osama Hussein Obama, having been the first Muslim Vice-President elected, now became the first Muslim president of the United States. The American era was over.

Taking advantage of the chaos in America and the political cowardice of the European leaders, Muslim leaders in Europe took advantage of the situation. Because one-half of the babies being born in Europe by 2013 were of Muslim descent, Muslim clerics demanded equal representation in the Parliaments throughout Europe and control of the European Union. Chaos reigned in Europe as well. The great riots of 2006 that took place in France were repeated in 2013, except this time all of Western Europe was under Marshal Law. Faced with economic collapse, the established order capitulated and Muslim leaders assumed control of the government, the educational institutions and the press. Majority memberships on the boards of European banks and trading companies, mining companies and auto manufacturers soon followed.

People throughout Europe, the United States and Africa clamored for a leader that espoused peace, unity and no more war. In the face of this global strife and chaos, the leader of Iran stepped forward calling for peace and an end to the senseless violence.

With the collapse of Iraq and the pullout of U.S. troops from that country in 2008, Iran had become the dominant player in the Middle East. It assumed control of not only the Iraqi but also the Saudi oil fields. The

Sh'ia clerics based in Iran now called the shots for their satellite countries of Egypt, Syria, Lebanon, Jordan, Iraq, Afghanistan, Saudi Arabia, Yemen, Ethiopia, Somalia and the Sudan.

The Supreme Spiritual Leader of Iran, Osama bin Laden, who had come out of hiding after the U.S. pullout of Iraq in 2008, declared that Muslim prophecy had been fulfilled. Bin Laden had become a Sh'ia Muslim, claiming he was actually the 12th Imam. He traveled to the United Nations in Copenhagen, which had been hastily located there after its headquarters was heavily damaged when the nuclear cruise missile exploded over Manhattan. When bin Laden spoke to the United Nations, as he would later report, he suddenly felt, "surrounded by light." A "light from heaven," he claimed. Later it was reported that when he began his speech in the name of 'Allah,' those present saw a light surround bin Laden, protecting him throughout his speech. Bin Laden would later recount, "Suddenly the atmosphere changed, and for the 30 minutes of my talk, the leaders assembled before me could not blink. All of the leaders sat motionless without blinking as if a hand held them and made them sit up and listen. They all had their eyes, ears and hearts open for the message from Allah, from the great Islamic Republic." Bin Laden stated that his mission had been fulfilled, that is, to "pave the path for the glorious reappearance of Imam Mahdi." The mystical 12th Imam of Sh'ia Islam, whose glorious return had been anticipated for over 1,000 years, was now ready to appear. He took the stage at the United Nations and indicated that he would reign on the earth for seven years, bringing about the last judgment upon all the infidels and upon all those who refused to convert to the last great religion, Islam.

All of the nations' populace were called upon to begin the conversion process to Islam or face the consequences. The new American President, Osama Hussein Obama, readily agreed. Most of the American people, facing unemployment, chaos, starvation and the end of life as they had known it, readily agreed.

By 2036, the last holdouts were the intolerant Christians of the old American South. By 2039, the Bible Belt rebellion had finally been put down and the world was now safe for Islam. Those that refused to accept Islam were either beheaded or forced into servitude working as second-class citizens, known as "dhimitude." Because the Christian rebellion had been so difficult to put down, as Christians were able to easily move in and out of their culture without being detected, in the year 2040, it was demanded that anyone who was not Christian be branded with a mark so that Christians could be easily distinguished. It was the natural next step of a policy that had begun in Iran in 2007. Then, all Jews in Iran were forced to wear yellow stars so that they could be easily identified, and all Christians were forced to wear red stars so that they could be easily identified. The world yawned, and so the policy was enacted. The Judeo-Christian era was over and planet Earth began a descent into a long, dark night.

## WAKE UP, AMERICA! WAKE UP JUDEO-CHRISTIANS! WAKE UP WESTERN CIVILIZATION!

Mark Steyn writes, "Permanence is the illusion of every age. In 1913 no one thought the Russian,

Austrian, German and Turkish empires would be gone within half a decade. Seventy years ago, all those who dismissed Reagan as an "amiable dunce" assured us that the Soviet Union was likewise here to stay. In 1987, there were no experts predicting the imminent fall of the Berlin Wall, the Warsaw pact countries or the U.S.S.R. itself."[lxxvii] And yet, all those things happened and supposedly nobody saw it coming. The clash of civilizations described in this book is coming and it's been on the march for some time.

How many times does a leader and a populace have to chant "Death to America! Death to Israel! and Death to the West" before our political leaders take note? Even *Newsweek* magazine, certainly not known for its conservative slant or bias, featured an article by Babak Dehghanpisheh and Christopher Dickey, entitled "The Next Nuclear Threat*"* in its February 13, 2006 issue.[lxxviii] The article states that Israeli intelligence suggests that a workable Iranian nuclear weapon may be only a year away. The article also went on to point out that not since the Ayatollah Khomeini was alive in the 1980's has Iran provoked so many regional and global tensions. "This is the war generation," said Massoud Denhmaki, a documentary filmmaker in Iran. The survivors of the savage battles between Iraq and Iran in the 1980's have now assumed political power. The younger generation now populating the schools have the attitude that "(A)n Islamic renaissance is starting from here…We are witnessing the start of a fundamentalist uprising in the region from the Muslim Brotherhood in Egypt to Hamas, Hezbollah and Mr. Ahmadinejad in our own country."[lxxix]

Mousa Abu Marzuk, deputy chief of Hamas' political bureau in Damascus, Syria, states that Hamas' political triumph in the Palestinian elections is an important springboard toward the Caliphate, a global Islamic state where life would be dictated by the Sharia.[lxxx]

The spiritual leader of Hamas, the late Ahmad Yassin, said, "The 21$^{st}$ century is the Century of Islam." His successor, Mamood Zahar, stated, "Israel will disappear and after it, the U.S."[lxxxi] Obviously, Hamas is not alone. Al Qaeda, Hezbollah and other radical Islamist organizations have openly stated, "We will turn the White House and the British Parliaments into mosques."[lxxxii]

And what the radical Islamists cannot achieve by violence, murder, mayhem and terror, they will achieve by political means and taking advantage of the political correctness of the values-neutered West. The global Jihadists of Islam will plant outposts in every nation around the world through their mosques. Once there, they will start the process of feeding as a parasite on their hosts until they achieve critical mass. Then begins the more serious task of subverting their host until they first have disproportionate influence and then total control.

Chapter 1 of this endeavor began with a discussion of what the reader is not being told about the "War on Terror." In this concluding chapter, you read why Osama bin Laden repeatedly vows to end 80 years of "humiliation and disgrace." It is because it has been about 80 years since the global Islamic empire of the

Turks was carved up and the holy lands of Allah were divided into Algeria, Libya, Morocco, Iraq, Iran, Syria, Egypt, Saudi Arabia and other countries designed to strip Islam of its military unity and its worldwide might.

You have not been told that one of Sunni Islam's top clerics, Shiek Yousef al-Qaradhawi, declares on one of his television programs that "Islam will return to Europe as a conqueror and victor." Then there is the Imam in Sudan, Mohammed Abd al-Karim who preaches that the "Prophet said that the Muslims would take India." You will not hear the Imam who presides over Saudi Arabia's mosque of King Fahd Defense Academy when he preaches, "We will control the land of the Vatican; we will control Rome and introduce Islam in it. Yes, the Christians, who carved crosses on the breasts of the Muslims in Kosovo and before them in Bosnia, and before them in many places in the world will yet pay us the jizya tax in humiliation or they will convert to Islam."[lxxxiii]

Those familiar with the Book of Revelation in the Christian Bible already know the answer. They know that it is not the 12th Imam that returns in glory. In what could be considered a rip-off of Christian writing, it is not the return of the 12th Imam, but the return of Jesus Christ to reign for a thousand years, which was written first and is found in the Christian Bible.

However, what is not told in the Book of Revelation is <u>when</u> the triumphant return will take place. It is entirely possible that the return may not occur until the world is governed by a Sh'ia Caliphate, and with it, intolerance, the degradation of women, the suppression of freedom of speech, freedom of thought, freedom of assembly and freedom of the press. Will the Antichrist of the Book of Revelation arise out of radical Islam? Since the Reformation and Renaissance, the development of Western political, economical and social thought has birthed societies and countries that have enabled its citizens to enjoy more freedom, more dignity, more prosperity and more advances in science and technology than any civilization in world history.

We in the West and moderate Muslims must therefore denounce the severing of hands and feet as punishment for theft; we must denounce the stoning to death of women as punishment for adultery; we must continue to strive for equality among all races, religions, colors, and ethnicity. We may have to fight once again for freedom of thought, belief and expression and the sacredness of all human life. In the short run, we must help reform radical Islam in the same way that Judaism and Christianity were reformed.

## WHAT MUST BE DONE.
### 1. Military policy
a. Stay the course in Iraq

A withdrawal from Iraq before the new democracy is ready to stand on its own would be catastrophic. In January of 2007, the United States military delivered proof that Iran is actively attempting to destabilize the new Iraqi government. Iran also supplied Hezbollah with the rockets that were launched from Lebanon into Israel. Iran is seeking to dominate the region. A strong, independent Iraq is crucial to maintaining a balance of power in that region to fend off the dominance of radical Sh'ia Islam in the Middle East. An aggressive radical Sh'ia Islam in control of the Middle East could lead to control by Iran of the oil fields, not only in Iraq, but in Kuwait and Saudi Arabia. Further, the probability that Iran will have nuclear capability in the very near term, means that it is imperative that Iran is held in check. A stable Iraq is the surest way to accomplish this.

b. Short of military intervention in Iran, which this writer does not advocate at this time, funds can be best spent by working with those citizens of Iran who do not subscribe to the radicalism of its current leadership. Unlike Saddam Hussein's Iraq, Iran has a long history of a more enlightened citizenry. Students, journalists, lawyers, businessmen and others have created pockets of resistance to the radical regime. This civil society could welcome a more secular and moderate form of government. As Kenneth R. Timmerman has written, it should become the official policy of the United States government to support regime change in Iran.[lxxxiv] But such a policy cannot be an unfunded mandate. The "Iran Freedom Support Act," introduced by Senator Rick Santorum in February of 2005 must not be allowed to die in the new Democrat congress.

Invoking the memory of Vietnam is not useful in evaluating the current conflict in Iraq. A radical

Sh'ia-dominated Afghanistan and Iraq allied with radical Iran presents a threat to the security and safety of the United States and us, its people. A communist Vietnam posed no such threat.

    c. Begin a national debate on how to position our military, in terms of troop deployment and how it should respond to a different kind of enemy than what the U. S. confronted in the Cold War, including whether re-instatement of the draft is a viable alternative.

## 2. Social and Economic Policy.

    a. We must demand of our leaders that we specifically identify the enemy against whom we fight. President Bush identified them as Islamic Fascists once, shortly after the 5$^{th}$ anniversary of the 9/11 attacks on the World Trade Center. Following the predictable round of criticisms by the Muslim apologist groups and the radical Muslim community, the administration backed off. Wrong! The American people must be informed, fearlessly and honestly, as to the threat that we face.

    b. We must reduce our dependence on foreign oil. 70% of proven oil reserves are in the Middle East, so it is utterly incomprehensible that Congress recently could not pass a bill to allow oil drilling in Alaska or in the Gulf of Mexico. We must increase our capacity to drill for and refine oil.

c. We must engage in an all-out effort to develop alternative fuel technologies.

We need a national Manhattan Project to end our dependence on the internal combustion engine as the chief mode of transportation and energy. This calls for a partnership between academia, government and industry. When the world buys Middle East or Venezuelan oil, the world funds terrorism and ultimately funds the purchase of the guns and the bullets and the bombs that will be used to kill them. Concurrently, the United States should drop its 53-cent-per-gallon tariff on Brazilian ethanol, at least until American farmers can catch up with our own domestic production.

d. End the ban on racial profiling in the context of airport screening. Our airliners were not commandeered by Swedes...

e. Secure our borders!
(i) Oppose and stop illegal immigration and limit legal immigration from Muslim nations.

Enact a sound national policy on the issuance of driver's licenses.

f. Increase funding for the Voice of America in the Middle East and for the purpose of helping moderate Muslims obtain a voice in Middle East affairs without fear of reprisal from the radicals.

**3. Our leaders should recognize that Western Europe is culturally much different than when those countries were our allies during the Cold War.** Mark Steyn wrote an article appearing in The New Criterion entitled "The Century Ahead—It's the Demography, Stupid." He states in clear and unmistakable terms that because of the low birth rate in Western European countries for the past thirty years, it's only a matter of time before the Muslim immigrant population literally takes over Europe. He writes:

> The latter half of the decline and fall of great civilizations follows a familiar pattern: Affluence, softness, decadence, extinction. You don't notice yourself slipping through those stages because usually there is a seductive politician on hand to provide the age with a sly self-deluding slogan like Bill Clinton's "its about the future of all of our children" but in some respects… Bill Clinton was right. A society that <u>has no children has no future</u>."[lxxxv]

And so we must create closer alliances with Eastern European countries and others that share our vision of freedom, individual responsibility and opportunity. We must throw off the blinders induced by Cold War alliances and realize that France and Germany may no longer be our trusted allies sharing a common heritage.

## 4. Marginalize the U.N.

The Oil-for- Food scandal should be enough to convince any fair minded individual that the United Nations is not the answer to this cataclysmic clash of civilizations.

## 5. We must embolden our leaders to raise the consciousness of all U. S. citizens about the threat we face.

Fear of being labeled "intolerant" paralyzes and stunts the speech of our politicians. *Note to politicians:* Truth is intolerant, but it's still true.

This awakening of America must be a grass roots effort. Our politicians will not listen or act unless we speak out and demand action from our leaders.

## CONCLUSION

We cannot wage a war (culturally or otherwise) against Islamofascists while:

Maintaining our dependence on foreign oil.

Turning a blind eye to Islamic destruction of Hindus, Christians and other "infidels" around the world; allowing mass immigration of Muslims and others into our own country.

Allowing "political correctness" to intimidate or blind us from recognizing and dealing with the threat we face.

Radical Islamists are militarily weak but ideologically strong. The West is militarily strong but ideologically weak and insecure.

In the end, the real problem facing Western Civilization is <u>not</u> how the Muslims might respond to a policy hostile to their interests, but whether the West still has the moral strength to adopt <u>any</u> policy short of political correctness.

What legacy will we leave our children?

Will we leave them the light and enlightenment of the Judeo-Christian ethic or a world of radical Muslim darkness for them to stumble through?

A people unwilling to die for their faith or country will die at the hands of a people who are.

Tell your friends and neighbors the threat is real and certain. The alarm bells will have to sound from the bottom up in order for our leaders to take action.

# BIBLIOGRAPHY

## BOOKS

1. *Eurabia: The Euro-Arab Axis,* by Bat Ye'or, Farleigh Dickinson University Press, 2005.

2. *Holy War on the Home Front,* by Harvey Kushner with Bart Davis, Sentinel Press, 2004.

3. *The Myth of Islamic Tolerance: How Islamic Law Treats Non-Muslims,* edited by Robert Spencer, Prometheus Books, 2005.

4. *The Sword of the Prophet,* by Serge Trifkovic, Regina Orthodox Press, Inc., 2002.

5. *War Footing: 10 Steps America Must Take to Prevail in the War for the Free  World,* by Frank J. Gaffney and Colleagues, Naval Institute Press, Annapolis, MD,  2006.

6. *The West's Last Chance,* by Tony Blankley, Regnery Publishing, Inc., 2005.

7. *Unholy Alliance: Radical Islam and the American Left,* by
 David  Horowitz, Regnery Publishing, Inc., 2004.

8. *The Case For Democracy*, by Natan Sharansky, Public Affairs ™, 2004.

9. *The Death of the West*, by Patrick J. Buchanan, Thomas Dunne Books, 2002.

10. *Bias*, by Bernard Goldberg, Regnery Publishing, Inc., 2002.

11. *While Europe Slept*, by Bruce Bawer, Doubleday, 2006.

12. *Slander*, by Ann Coulter, Three Rivers Press, 2002.

13. *Treason*, by Ann Coulter, Crown Forum, 2003.

14. *Menace in Europe*, by Claire Berlinski, Crown Forum, 2006.

15. *The Force of Reason,* by Oriana Fallaci, Rizzoli International Publications, Inc., 2004.

16. *The Religions Next Door,* by Marvin Ovasky, Broadman and Holman Publishers, 2004.

17. *Future Jihad,* by Walid Phares, Palgrave Macmillan, 2005.

18. *The Far Enemy,* by Fawaz A. Gerges, Cambridge University Press, 2005.

19. *The Politically Incorrect Guide to Islam,* by Robert Spencer, Regnery Publishing, Inc., 2005.

20. *Islamic Imperialism,* by Efraim Karsh, Yale University Press, 2006.

21. T*he Criminalization of Christianity,* by Janet L. Folger, Multnomah Publishers Inc., 2005.

22. *A Countdown to Crisis,* by Kenneth R. Timmerman, Three Rivers Press, Inc., 2005, 2006.

23. *Now they Call me Infidel,* by Nonie Darwish, The Penguin Group, Inc., 2006.

24. *Holy War on the Home Front,* by Harvey Kushner, The Penguin Group, Inc., 2004.

25. *America Alone*, by Mark Steyn, Regnery Publishing, Inc., 2006.

26. *The War for Muslim Minds,* by Gilles Kepel, First Harvard University Press, 2004.

27. *Islam Unveiled,* by Robert Spencer, Encounter Books, 2002.

28. *The Truth about Muhammad* by Robert Spencer, Regnery Publishing, Inc., 2006.

29. *The Looming Tower,* by Lawrence Wright, Alfred A. Knopf, 2006.

30. *Because They Hate,* by Brigitte Gabriel, New York St. Martin's Press, 2006.

31. *What the Koran Really Says,* by Ibn Warraq, Amherst New York Prometheus  Books, 2002.

32. *No god but God*, by Reza Aslan, (New York, Random House, 2005)

**ARTICLES**

1. "The Century Ahead," by Mark Steyn, article appeared in *The New Criterion,* January, 2006.

2. "How to Topple the Mullahs," by Kenneth R. Timmerman, *FrontPage Magazine.com,* January 18, 2007.

3. "The Covenant of the Islamic Resistant Movement (Hamas)," *Mideast Web historical documents,* August 18, 1988.
4. "The New Berlin Wall," by Peter Schneider, article appeared in *The New York Times Magazine*, December 4, 2005.

5. "A Lawyer's Perspective on the Iraq War," by Raymond S. Kraft.

6. "Chronology of Prophet Muhammad," cartoon controversy, *FoxNews.com,* February 6, 2006.

7. "Editorial Cartoon," by Dianne Rinehart, *The Hamilton Spectator,* February 4, 2006.

8. "Cleric: Bombings Sign from God," *FoxNews.com,* November 18, 2005.

9. "NATO troops open fire on Afghan demonstrators," *FoxNews.com,* February 7, 2006.

10. "The World at Civil War," by Suzanne Fields, *townhall.com,* March 23, 2006.

11. "Making Babies in Berlin," by Suzanne Fields, *townhall.com,* March 27, 2006.

12. "The Islamic Threat is Greater than German and Soviet Threats Were," by Dennis Prager, *townhall.com,* March 28, 2006.

13. "The Clash of World Views," by Charles Colson, April 4, 2006. *Breakpoint.org*

14. "The Caliphate is Coming," by Rachel Ehrenfeld, *frontpagemagazine.com,* January 31, 2006.

15. "Muslims Target U.S. Embassy in Indonesia," *FoxNews.com,* February 19, 2006.

16. "Subsidizing the Enemy," by Daniel Pipes, *frontpagemagazine.com,* April 28, 2006.

17. "Knowing the Enemy," by George Packer, *The New Yorker Magazine,* December 18, 2006.
18. "My Response to Dinesh D'Souza," by Robert Spencer, *frontpagemagazine.com,* January 22, 2007.

19. "The Century Ahead," by Mark Steyn, *The New Criterion,* January, 2006.

20. "The Visiting Jihadist," by Joe Kaufman, *frontpagemagazine.com,* March 17, 2006.

21. "Muslim Bites Dog," by Ann Coulter, *townhall.com,* February 15, 2006.

22. "Menaced Holy Land Christians," by Robert Novak, *townhall.com,* February 16, 2006.

23. "Why I Published Those Cartoons," by Flemming Rose, *Washingtonpost.com,* February 19, 2006.

24. "Islamic Radicals Take Advantage of Western Liberalism," by John Leo, *townhall.com,* February 12, 2006.

25. "Submission is all in your Dhimitude," by Diana West, *townhall.com,* February 13, 2006.

26. "From Hitler to Hamas," by Suzanne Fields, *townhall.com,* February 6, 2006.

27. "Hometown Jihad," by Patrick Poole, *frontpagemag.com,* April 3, 2006.

28. "Afghan Man Faces Death for Allegedly Converting to Christianity,"

30. "Devoted and Defiant," by Babak Dehghanpisheh and Christopher Dickey, *Newsweek Magazine,* February 13, 2006.

# ENDNOTES

## CHAPTER 1

i   Tony Blankley, *The West's Last Chance,* Regnery Publishing, Inc., 2005.

ii  Ibid.

iii Ibid.

iv  *South Florida Sun-Sentinel,* November 25, 2005.

v   *South Florida Sun-Sentinel,* December 31, 2005.

vi  Bat Ye'or, *Eurabia,* Fairleigh Dickinson University Press, 2005.

vii foxnews.com, "Violence Creates Terror in Indonesia," Associated Press, December 26, 2005.

viii Remarks attributed to Mahmoud Ahmadinejad at, "A World Without Zionism Conference," October 26, 2005.

ix  Ibid.

x     See also, AmericanCongressforTruth.com,
      Brigitte Gabriel, Founder.

xi    See Note 1.

xii   Adapted from quotes attributed to Ann Coulter
      as reported in Associated Press articles appear-
      ing in *South Florida Sun-Sentinel,* February,
      2006.

xiii  Found on AmericanCongressforTruth.com,
      Brigitte Gabriel, Founder.

**CHAPTER 2**

xiv   Mark Steyn, *America Alone,* Regnery
      Publishing, Inc., 2006.

xv    Peter Schneider, "The New Berlin Wall, *New
      York Times Magazine,* December 4, 2005.

xvi   Ibid.

xvii  Adapted from quotes attributed to Theodore
      Roosevelt found on TheodoreRoosevelt.com.

xviii See Note 2.

xix   Ayaan Hirsi Ali now lives in Washington, DC
      and works for the American Enterprise
      Institute.

xx    Such quotes were obtained from websites
      such as Jihadwatch.com. Such quotes were
      not figured prominently in the western press.

xxi   Claire Berlinski, *Menace in Europe,* Crown
      Publishers, 2006.

xxii  Ibid.

xxiii Ibid.

xxiv  Ibid.

## CHAPTER 3

xxv    First reported at Foxnews.com, "Afghan Man Faces Death for Allegedly Converting to Christianity" Associated Press, March 19, 2006

xxvi    Robert Spencer, ed., *The Myth of Islamic Tolerance,* Prometheus Books, 2005.

xxvii    Ibid..

xxviii    Serge Trifkovic, *The Sword of the Prophet,* Regina Orthodox Press, 2002

xxix    Ibid.

xxx    Ibid.

xxxi    Efraim Karsh, *Islamic Imperialism,* Yale University Press, 2006.

xxxii    See Note 4.

xxxiii    See Note 4.

xxxiv    See Note 4.

xxxv    Oriana Fallaci, *The Force of Reason,* New York, Rizzoli International Publications, Inc., 2004.

## CHAPTER 4

xxxvi    Bernard Goldberg, *Bias,* Regnery Publishing, Inc. 2002.

xxxvii    Ibid.

xxxviii    Ibid.

xxxix    Ibid.

xl    Ibid

xli    Ibid.

xlii    Ibid.

xliii    David Horowitz, *Unholy Alliance,* Washington, D.C. Regnery Publishing Inc., 2004

xliv    Ibid.
xlv     Ibid.
xlvi    Ibid.
xlvii   Ibid.
xlviii  Alexis de Tocqueville, *Democracy In America,* Gerald Bevan Translator, New York, Penguin Classics, 2003.
xlix    Adapted from *Tribes,* published on ejecte-jecteject.com, September 5, 2005.

## CHAPTER 5

1       Harvey Kushner, *Holy War on the Home Front,* Penguin Group, New York, 2004.
li      Ibid.
lii     Ibid.
liii    Ibid.
liv     Ibid.
lv      Ibid.
lvi     Interview with former F.B.I. agent who wishes to remain anonymous.
lvii    See Note 1.
lviii   Ibid.
lix     Ibid.
lx      Ibid.
lxi     Ibid.
lxii    Ibid.
lxiii   Ibid.
lxiv    Ibid.
lxv     Ibid.

## CHAPTER 6

lxvi    Author unknown.
lxvii   Oriana Fallaci, *The Force of Reason,* Rizzoli
        International Publications, Inc., 2004.
lxviii  Janet L. Folger, *The Criminilization
        Criminalization of Christianity*, Sisters
        Press, Multnomah Publishers, Oregon, 2005.
lxix    Ibid.
lxx     Ibid.
lxxi    Ibid.
lxxii   Ibid.

## CHAPTER 7

lxxiii  Remarks delivered by U.S. Senator Rick
        Santorum at the National Press Club, July 20,
        2006.
lxxiv   Kenneth R. Timmerman, *Countdown to Crisis,*
        Three Rivers Press, New York, 2005.
lxxv    Adapted from a website known as,
        r*epublicworldnews.com.*